Meditations
Marcus Aurelius
17th century translation by Méric Casaubon
Edited for the modern reader by Stephen McGrew

Other books by McGrew:

Nobots
Mars, Ho!
Voyage to Earth
Yesterday's Tomorrows (out of print)
The Paxil Diaries
Random Scribblings
Grandma's Cookbook

ISBN 978-0-9910531-8-6
Printed in the United States of America

A very big thanks to Wikipedia, where all of the illustrations came from, and from where I plagiarized most of the notes.

Table of Contents

Foreword

This project was originally going to be a quick and dirty easy task, like all the other books I host that are written by others. It was prompted by seeing something about the "plague emperor". I would simply open the book at Gutenberg, copy it, format it, and post it. Unfortunately, the version at Gutenberg would be completely unreadable to most modern readers.

The original version was written in Greek. It was translated to English in the early seventeenth century by Méric Casaubon, so the verbiage is very antiquated and impossible to understand by most modern readers, so I have edited it, changing "thou" to "you" along with other similar antiquated words.

Reading the original translation required numerous trips to a dictionary, because there are a lot of words that haven't been written or spoken in centuries. Some of the words weren't even in any dictionary, and looking for them in Google led me only to this book, so I had to figure it out; I found that many times, what was once spelled with an "E" is now spelled with a "T". It was hard to figure out that "eareh" was actually "earth", and "woryer" was actually "worthy"; it was like deciphering some sort of code. I've also given it a more modern structure while leaving a feeling of quaintness.

I suspect that the copy that I got from Gutenberg (http://www.gutenberg.org/files/55317/55317-h/55317h.htm) was OCRed and its output wasn't edited at all, as some places seemed to have OCR errors (I have since returned, Gutenberg had a site redesign and that URL is no longer good, replaced by a better copy).

The quick and dirty has so far taken months, and is nowhere near finished as I write this. Little is exactly as it was; I have made it mine.

I had hoped to make this not only readable, but a good read. Unfortunately, that's incredibly difficult. There were no paragraphs, with many places having walls of text spanning pages. There are redundancies that would change the character of the book if fixed. There are sentences that are way too long. I have split most of the run-on sentences, but as I write this it appears that many would have to be left as is. Marcus Aurelius himself said he was deficient in writing and oratory. However, I have done the best I could, and it is no longer unreadable, and possibly enjoyable. I found it interesting.

Marcus Aurelius was Emperor of Rome from 161 AD to his death in 180. During his reign a horrible plague struck Europe, a plague that bears his name. As I write this, a plague named Covid-19 has ravaged the planet, killing more people in America than died in all of the wars we've been in since Korea, with the death toll now rising every day, and shut down most of the world's economy, throwing millions of people out of work.

His father died when he was three, and his mother and grandfather raised him.

Marcus Aurelius was known as a "philosopher king". He was a Pagan, like most people of the time, but still thought well of the Christian God, although not the Christians themselves. Before he was emperor, when he was a captain in charge of an infantry, his whole command was dying of thirst and a Christian prayed that God ease their suffering, and it rained heavily. Under his rule, the national persecution of Christians was stopped, although regional persecution was still permitted.

His philosophy was stoicism, which comes in handy during a pandemic. This book is almost certainly where the character of Mister Spock, and his fellow Vulcans, come from in the *Star Trek* shows. This is Vulcan philosophy, even though Vulcans are fiction.

These writings were notes to himself, not for publication, but as it was written by a philosopher during a plague, although I disagree with much of it, it contains wisdom and you may find it worthwhile.

In several places he notes that nothing ever changes even though everything changes. In his time that was obvious and true, people lived then just as they had lived a millennium earlier. Change that was noticeable in a single human lifetime didn't occur until the Renaissance.

Chapter One
The Teachers

From my grandfather Verus I have learned to be gentle and meek, and to refrain from all anger and passion. From the fame and memory of him that begot me I have learned both modesty and manlike behavior.

Of my mother I have learned to be religious, and bountiful. To forbear, not only to do, but to intend any evil, to content myself with a spare diet, and to flee all such excess as is incidental to great wealth.

Of my great-grandfather, both to frequent public schools and auditoriums, and to get me good and able teachers at home, and that I ought not to think much, if upon such occasions, I were at excessive charges.

▼

Of him that brought me up, not to be fondly addicted to either of the two great factions of the coursers in the circus, called *Prasini*, and *Veneti*. Nor in the amphitheater partially to favor any of the gladiators, or fencers, as either the *Parmularii*, or the *Secutores*.

Moreover, to endure labor, nor to need many things. When I have anything to do, to do it myself rather than by others. Not to meddle with many businesses, and not easily to admit of any slander.

▼

Of Diognetus[1], not to busy myself about vain things, and not to easily believe those things which are commonly spoken by such as take upon themselves to work wonders, and by sorcerers, or prestidigitators, and impostors. Concerning the power of charms, and their driving out of demons, or evil spirits and the like.

Not to keep quails for the game; nor to be crazy for such things. Not to be offended with other men's freedom of speech, and to apply myself to philosophy.

4

Him also I must thank, that ever I heard first Bacchius, then Tandasis and Marcianus, and that I wrote dialogues in my youth; and that I took liking to the philosophers' little couch and skins, and such other things which by the Grecian discipline are proper to those who profess philosophy.

▼

To Rusticus[2] I am beholden that I first entered into the conceit that my life wanted some redress and cure. And then, that I did not fall into the ambition of ordinary sophists[3], either to write tracts concerning the common theorems, or to exhort men to virtue and the study of philosophy by public orations. Also that I never by way of ostentation affected to show myself an active able man, for any kind of bodily exercises.

That I gave over the study of rhetoric and poetry, and of elegant, neat language. That I did not use to walk about the house in my long robe, nor to do any such things. Moreover I learned of him to write letters without any affectation, or curiosity; such as that was by him was written to my mother from Sinuessa.

To be easy and ready to be reconciled, and well pleased again with them that had offended me, as soon as any of them would be content to seek to me again. To read with diligence, not to rest satisfied with a light and superficial knowledge, nor quickly to assent to things commonly spoken of, whom I must also thank that I ever lighted upon Epictetus his *Hypomnemata*, or moral commentaries and common-factions, which also he gave me of his own.

▼

From Apollonius[4], true liberty, invariable steadfastness, and not to regard anything at all, though never so little but right and reason. Always, whether in the sharpest pains or after the loss of a child or in long diseases, to be still the same man who also was a present and visible example to me, that it was possible for the same man to be both vehement and remiss.

A man not subject to be vexed and offended with the incapacity of his scholars and auditors in his lectures and expositions. A true pattern of a man who of all his good gifts and faculties, least esteemed in himself that his excellent skill and ability to teach and persuade others the common theorems and maxims of the Stoic philosophy.

Of him also I learned how to receive favors and kindnesses (as commonly they are accounted) from friends, so that I might not become obnoxious to them, for them, nor more yielding upon occasion, than in right I should, yet so that I should not pass them either, as an insensible and unthankful man.

▼

From Sextus[5], mildness and the pattern of a family governed with paternal affection, and a purpose to live according to nature. To be grave without affectation. To observe carefully the several dispositions of my friends and not to be offended with idiots, nor unseasonably to set upon those that are carried with vulgar opinions.

With theorems, and tenets of philosophers, his conversation being an example how a man might accommodate himself to all men and companies, so that though his company were sweeter and more pleasing than any flatterer's plagiarism and fawning, yet at the same time it was most respected and reverenced who also had a proper happiness and faculty.

Rationally and methodically to find out, and set in order all necessary determinations and instructions for a man's life. A man without ever the least appearance of anger, or any other passion. Able at the same time most exactly to observe the Stoic *Apathia*, or dispassionateness, and yet to be most tender hearted. Ever of good credit, and yet almost without any noise, or rumor. Very learned, and yet making little show.

▼

From Alexander the Grammarian, to be un-reprovable myself, and not reproachfully to reprehend any man for a barbarism, or a solecism, or any false pronunciation. Rather, dexterously by way of answer, or testimony, or confirmation of the same matter (taking no notice of the word) to utter it as it should have been spoken, or by some other such close and indirect admonition, handsomely and civilly telling him of it.

▼

From Fronto[6], to how much envy and fraud and hypocrisy the state of a tyrannous king is subject to, and how they who are commonly called "nobly born", are in some sort incapable or void of natural affection.

▼

Of Alexander the Platonic, seldom and only when in great need say, or to write to any man in a letter, "I am not at leisure." Nor in this manner still to put off those duties, which we owe to our friends and acquaintances (to every one in his kind) under pretense of urgent affairs.

▼

From Catulus, not to contemn any friend's expostulation, even though unjust, but to strive to reduce him to his former disposition, freely and heartily to speak well of all my masters upon any occasion, as it is reported of Domitius, and Athenodotus; and to love my children with true affection.

▼

From my brother Severus, to be kind and loving to all them of my house and family. By him I also came to the knowledge of Thrasea and Helvidius, and Cato, and Dio, and Brutus. It was also he that put me in the first conceit and desire of an equal commonwealth, administered by justice and equality.

Of a kingdom that should regard no more than the good

and welfare of the subjects. Of him also, to observe a constant tenor (not interrupted, with any other cares and distractions), in the study and esteem of philosophy.

To be bountiful and liberal in the largest measure, always to hope the best, and to be confident that my friends love me. In whom I moreover observed open dealing towards those whom he reproved at any time, and that his friends might without all doubt or much observation know what he would, or wouldn't do, so open and plain he was.

▼

From Claudius Maximus[7], in all things endeavor to have power over myself, and in nothing to be carried about. To be cheerful and courageous in all sudden chances and accidents, as in sicknesses. To love mildness, and moderation, and gravity. To do my business, whatever it is, thoroughly, and without complaining.

Whatever he said, all men believed him that as he spake, so he thought, and whatever he did, that he did it with a good intent. His manner was to never wonder at anything; never to be in a hurry, and yet never be slow. Nor to be perplexed, or dejected, or at any time unseemly, or excessively laugh; nor to be angry, or suspicious.

Ever ready to do good, and to forgive, and to speak truth. And all this, as one that seemed rather of himself to have been straight and right, than ever to have been rectified or redressed. Neither was there any man that ever thought himself undervalued by him, or that could find in his heart to think himself a better man than he. He would also be very pleasant and gracious.

In my father, I observed his meekness, and his constancy without wavering in those things which after a due examination and deliberation he had determined. How free from all vanity he carried himself in matter of honor and dignity, (as they are esteemed) his laboriousness and assiduity, his readiness to hear any man that had anything to say tending to any common good.

How generally and impartially he would give every man his due. His skill and knowledge, when rigor or extremity, or when remissness or moderation was in season. How he abstained from all unchaste love of youths. His moderate condescending to other men's occasions as an ordinary man, neither absolutely requiring of his friends that they should wait upon him at his ordinary meals, nor that they should of necessity accompany him in his journeys.

That whenever any business upon some necessary occasions was to be put off and omitted before it could be ended, he was ever found when he went about it, again the same man that he was before. His accurate examination of things in consultations, and patient hearing of others.

He would not easily give over the search of the matter, as one easy to be satisfied with sudden notions and apprehensions. His care to preserve his friends; how neither at any time he would carry himself towards them with disdainful neglect, and grow weary of them, nor yet at any time be madly fond of them.

His mind was contented in all things, his cheerful countenance, his care to foresee things far off, and to take order for the least, without any noise or clamor. Moreover how all acclaim and flattery were repressed by him.

How carefully he observed all things necessary to the government, and kept an account of the common expenses, and how patiently he would abide that he was reprehended by some for this his strict and rigid kind of dealing. How he was neither a superstitious worshiper of the gods, nor an ambitious pleaser of men, or studious of popular applause; but sober in all things, and everywhere observant of that which was fitting.

He was no affecter of novelties. In those things which conduced to his ease and convenience (plenty where his fortune afforded him), without pride and bragging, yet with all freedom and liberty, so that as he freely enjoyed them without any anxiety or affectation when they were present.

When absent, he found no want of them. Moreover, that he was never commended by any man, as either a learned acute man, or an fawning officious man, or a fine orator; but as a ripe mature man, a perfect sound man. One that could not endure to be flattered. One able to govern both himself and others.

Moreover, how much he honored all true philosophers, without upbraiding those that were not so. His sociability, his gracious and delightful conversation, but never to satiety.

His care of his body within bounds and measure, not as one that desired to live long, or over-studious of neatness, and elegance, and yet not as one that did not regard it, so that through his own care and providence he seldom needed any inward physic, or outward applications.

Especially how ingeniously he would yield to any that had obtained any peculiar faculty, as either eloquence, or the knowledge of the laws, or of ancient customs, or the like. How he concurred with them, in his best care and endeavor that every one of them might in his kind, for in that which he excelled was regarded and esteemed, and although he did all things carefully after the ancient customs of his forefathers, yet even of this was he was not desirous that men should take notice, that he imitated ancient customs.

Again, how he was not easily moved and tossed up and down, but loved to be constant, both in the same places and businesses. How after his great fits of headache he would return fresh and vigorous to his wonted affairs.

Again, that he neither had many secrets, nor often, and such only as concerned public matters. His discretion and moderation, in exhibiting of the public sights and shows for the pleasure and pastime of the people, in public buildings, presents, and the like.

In all these things, having a respect to men only as men, and to the equity of the things themselves, and not to the glory that might follow. Never wont to use the baths at unseasonable hours. No builder; never curious, or solicitous, either about his food, or about the workmanship, or color of his clothes, or about anything that belonged to external beauty.

In all his conversation, far from all inhumanity, all boldness, and incivility, all greediness and impetuosity. Never doing anything with such earnestness, and intention, that a man could say of him that he sweated about it. On the contrary, all things distinctly, as at leisure, without trouble. Orderly, soundly, and agreeably.

A man might have applied that to him, which is recorded of Socrates, that he knew how to want, and to enjoy those things. In the want whereof, most men show themselves weak. In the fruition, intemperate, but to hold out firm and constant, and to keep within the compass of true moderation and sobriety in either estate. This is proper to a man who has a perfect and invincible soul, such as he showed himself in the sickness of Maximus.

▼

From the gods I received that I had good grandfathers, and parents, a good sister, good masters, good domestics, loving kinsmen, almost all that I have; and that I never through hurry and rashness transgressed against any of them. Notwithstanding that my disposition was such that such a thing (if occasion had been) might very well have been committed by me, but that It was the mercy of the gods to prevent such a concurring of matters and occasions as might make me to incur this blame.

11

That I was not long brought up by the concubine of my father; that I preserved the flower of my youth. That I took not upon me to be a man before my time, but rather put it off longer than I needed. That I lived under the government of my lord and father, who would take away from me all prideful vanity. To reduce me to that conceit and opinion that it was not impossible for a prince to live in the court without a troop of guards and followers, extraordinary apparel, such and such torches and statues, and other like particulars of state and magnificence.

A man may reduce and contract himself almost to the state of a private man, and yet for all that not to become the more base and remiss in those public matters and affairs, wherein power and authority is requisite.

That I have had such a brother, who by his own example might stir me up to think of myself. By his respect and love, delighted and pleased me.

That I have got ingenuous children, and that they had no birth defects, nor with any other natural deformity. That I was not greatly proficient in the study of rhetoric and poetry, and of other faculties which perchance I might have dwelt upon, if I had found myself to go on in them with success.

That I did by times prefer those by whom I was brought up to such places and dignities that they seemed to me to desire the most, and that I didn't put them off with hope and expectation, that (since they were still young) I would do the same afterwards.

That I ever knew Apollonius and Rusticus, and Maximus. That I have often and effectually had occasion to consider and meditate with myself concerning that life which is according to nature what the nature and manner of it is; so that as for the gods and such suggestions, helps, and inspirations as might be expected from them, nothing hindered, but that I might have begun long before to live according to nature. Or that even now that I was not yet a partaker and in present possession of that life that I myself (in that I did not observe those inward motions, and suggestions. Yea, and almost plain and apparent instructions and admonitions of the gods), was the only cause of it.

That my body in such a life has been able to hold out so long. That I never had to do with Benedicta and Theodotus, yea and afterwards when I fell into some fits of love, I was soon cured.

That having been often displeased with Rusticus, I never did him anything for which afterwards I had occasion to repent. That it being so that my mother was to die young, yet she lived with me all her latter years.

That as often as I had a purpose to help and succor any that either were poor, or fallen into some present necessity, I never was answered by my officers that there was not ready money enough to do it. That I myself never had occasion to require the same assistance and help from any other.

That I have such a wife, so obedient, so loving, so ingenuous. That I had choice of fit and able men to whom I might commit the bringing up of my children. That by dreams I have received help, as for other things, so in particular how I might stay my casting of blood and cure my dizziness, as that also that happened to your in Cajeta, as to Chryses when he prayed by the seashore.

And when I first applied myself to philosophy, that I did not fall into the hands of some sophists, or spent my time either in reading the manifold volumes of ordinary philosophers, nor in practicing myself in the solution of arguments and fallacies, nor dwelt upon the studies of the meteors, and other natural curiosities. All these things without the assistance of the gods, and fortune, could not have been.

▼

Sometimes in the morning say to yourself, This day I will have to deal with an idle curious man, with an unthankful man, a complainer, a crafty, false, an envious man, or an unsociable uncharitable man. All these ill qualities have happened to them through ignorance of that which is truly good and truly bad.

But I that understand the nature of that which is good, that it only is to be desired, and of that which is bad, that it only is truly odious and shameful. Who knows moreover, that this transgressor, whoever he be, is my kinsman, not by the same blood and seed, but by participation of the same reason, and of the same divine particle.

How can I either be hurt by any of those, since it is not in their power to make me incur anything that is truly reproachful? Or angry, and ill affected towards him who by nature is so near to me? For we are all born to be fellow-workers, as the feet, the hands, and the eyelids; as the rows of the upper and under teeth. For such therefore to be in opposition, is against nature; and what is it to chafe at, and to be averse from, but to be in opposition?

▼

Whatever I am is either flesh, or life, or that which we commonly call the mistress and overruling part of man: reason. Away with your books, don't suffer your mind any more to be distracted and carried to and fro; for it will not be; but as even now ready to die, think little of your flesh. Blood, bones, and a skin; a pretty piece of knit and twisted work, consisting of nerves, veins and arteries; think no more of it, than that.

And as for your life, consider what it is; a wind; not one constant wind either, but every moment of an hour let out, and sucked in again.

The third is your ruling part, and here consider that you are an old man. Don't let that excellent part be brought in subjection and to become slavish. Don't put up with it to be drawn up and down with unreasonable and unsociable lusts and motions, as it were with wires and nerves.

Don't suffer from it any more, either to mope at anything now present, or to fear and fly from anything to come, which destiny has appointed to you.

▼

Whatever proceeds from the gods immediately that any man will grant totally depends from their divine providence. As for those things that are commonly said to happen by fortune, even those must be conceived to have dependence from nature, or from that first and general connection, and concatenation of all those things which are administered and brought to pass more apparently by divine providence.

All things flow from there. Whatever it is that is, is both necessary, and conducing to the whole (part of which you are), and whatever it is that is requisite and necessary for the preservation of the general, must of necessity for every particular nature be good and beneficial.

And as for the whole, it is preserved, as by the perpetual mutation and conversion of the simple elements one into another, so also by the mutation, and alteration of things mixed and compounded. Let these things suffice you; let them be always to you, as your general rules and precepts. As for your thirst after books, away with it with all speed, that you not die murmuring and complaining, but truly meek and well satisfied, and from your heart thankful to the gods.

▲

Chapter Two
The Mind

Remember how long you had already put off these things, and how often a certain day and hour as it were, having been set to you by the gods, you had neglected it. It is high time for you to understand the true nature both of the world, where you are a part, and of that Lord and Governor of the world, from whom, as a channel from the spring you yourself did flow, and that there is but a certain limit of time appointed to you. If you do not make use of it to calm and allay the many distempers of your soul, it will pass away and you with it, and will return never afterwards.

▼

Let it be your earnest and incessant care as a Roman and a man to perform whatever it is that you are about. Do it with true and unfeigned gravity, natural affection, freedom, and justice. And as for all other cares and imaginations, how you may ease your mind of them.

You will do this if you go about every action as your last action, free from all vanity, all passionate and willful aberration from reason, and from all hypocrisy, and self-love, and dislike of those things which by the fates or appointment of God have happened to you.

You see that those things, which for a man to hold on in a prosperous course and to live a divine life, are requisite and necessary. They are not many, for the gods will require no more of any man that shall but keep and observe these things.

▼

Do, soul, do; abuse and contemn yourself yet a while, and the time for you to respect yourself will be at an end. Every man's happiness comes from himself, but if you see your life is almost at an end while affording yourself no respect, you will make your happiness consist in the souls and conceits of other men.

▼

Why should any of these things that happen externally distract you so much? Give yourself leisure to learn some good things, and cease roving and wandering to and fro.

You must also take heed of another kind of wandering, for they are idle in their actions who toil and labor in this life who have no certain scope to direct all their motions and desires.

▼

For not observing the state of another man's soul, scarce was ever any man known to be unhappy.

Tell whoever that don't intend, and don't guide, by reason and discretion the motions of their own souls that they must of necessity be unhappy.

▼

These things you must always have in mind: What is the nature of the universe, and what is mine. In particular, what relation does this have to that? What kind of part, of what kind of universe it is? And that there is nobody that can hinder you, but that you may always both do and speak those things which are agreeable to that nature of which you are a part.

▼

Theophrastus, where he compares sin with sin (as after a vulgar sense such things I grant may be compared) says well and like a philosopher, that those sins are greater which are committed through lust, than those which are committed through anger.

For whoever is angry seems with a kind of grief and close contraction of themselves, to turn away from reason. But whoever sins through lust, being overcome by pleasure, does in his very sin a more impotent, and unmanly disposition.

Well then and like a philosopher does he say, that he of the two is the more to be condemned, that sins with pleasure, than he that sins with grief. For indeed this latter may seem first to have been wronged, and so in some manner through grief thereof to have been forced to be angry, whereas he who

17

through lust does commit anything, did of himself merely resolve upon that action.

▼

Whatever you affect, whatever you project, do so, and so project all, as one who (for you should know) may at this very present depart out of this life. And as for death, if there are any gods, it is no grievous thing to leave the society of men. The gods will do you no harm, you may be sure.

But if it is that there are no gods, or that they take no care of the world, why should I desire to live in a world void of gods, and of all divine providence? But there certainly are gods, and they take care of the world. As for those things which are truly evil, as vice and wickedness, such things they have put in a man's own power that he might avoid them if he would. Had there been anything besides that had been truly bad and evil, they would have had a care of that also, that a man might have avoided it.

But why should that be thought to hurt and prejudice a man's life in this world which cannot in any way make man himself better or worse in his own person? Neither must we think that the nature of the universe either through ignorance pass these things, or if not as ignorant of them, yet as unable either to prevent, or better to order and dispose them.

It cannot be that she through want either of power or skill, should have committed such a thing, so as to suffer all things both good and bad, equally and promiscuously, to happen to all both good and bad.

As for life therefore, and death, honor and dishonor, labor and pleasure, riches and poverty, all these things happen to men indeed, both good and bad equally. But as things which of themselves are neither good nor bad, because of themselves, neither shameful nor worthy of praise.

▼

Consider how quickly all things are dissolved and resolved. The bodies and substances themselves, into the matter and substance of the world. Their memories into the general age and time of the world.

Consider the nature of all worldly sensible things; especially those which either ensnare by pleasure, or for their irksomeness are dreadful, or for their outward luster and show are in great esteem and request. How vile and contemptible, how base and corruptible, how destitute of all true life and being they are!

▼

It is the part of a man who is endowed with a good understanding faculty to consider what they themselves are, from whose bare conceits and voices honor and credit proceed. As also what it is to die, and how if a man shall consider this by itself alone, to die, and separate from it in his mind all those things which with it usually represent themselves to us. He can conceive of it no other way than as of a work of nature, and he that fears any work of nature is childish. Now death is not only a work of nature, but also conducing to nature.

▼

Consider with yourself how man, and by what part of him is joined to God, and how that part of man is affected when it is said to be diffused. There is nothing more wretched than that soul which in a kind of circuit compasses all things, searching (as he said) even the very depths of the earth.

And by all signs and conjectures prying into the very thoughts of other men's souls, and yet this is not sensible that it's sufficient for a man to apply himself wholly, and to confine all his thoughts and cares to the tendency of that spirit which is within him, and truly and really to serve him.

His service consists in this, that a man keep himself pure from all violent passion and evil affection, from all rashness and vanity, and from all manner of discontent, either in regard of the gods or men. For indeed whatever proceeds from the gods deserves respect for their worth and excellency. Whatever proceeds from men, as they are our kinsmen, should by us be entertained with love, always.

Sometimes, it is as proceeding from their ignorance of

that which is truly good and bad, (a blindness, no less, than that by which we are not able to discern between white and black) with a kind of pity and compassion also.

▼

If you should live three thousand, or as many as ten thousand years, remember that man can not part with his life properly, except for that little part of life in which he now lives, and that which he lives is no other than that which at every instant he parts with. That, then, which is the longest of duration and that which is the shortest both come to one effect.

For although in regard of that which is already past there may be some inequality, yet that time which is now present and in being is equal to all men. And that being it which we part with whenever we die, it manifestly appears that it can be but a moment of time that we then part with.

For as for that which is either past or to come, a man cannot be said properly to part with it. For how should a man part with that which he has not?

These two things therefore you must remember. First, that all things in the world from all eternity, by a perpetual revolution of the same times and things ever continued and renewed, are of one kind and nature. Whether for a hundred or two hundred years only, or for an infinite space of time, a man sees those things which are still the same, it can be no matter of great moment.

And secondly, that that life which any the oldest, or the youngest parts with, is for length and duration the very same, for that only which is present is that which either of them can lose, as being that only which they have. That which he doesn't have no man can truly be said to lose.

▼

Remember that everything is only opinion and conceit, for those things are plain and apparent which were spoken to Monimus the Cynic; and as plain and apparent is the use that may be made of those things, if that which is true and serious

20

in them is received as well as that which is sweet and pleasing.

▼

A man's soul does wrong and disrespects itself first and especially when he lies. It becomes an abscess, as it were; a pimple of the world. It becomes a thing to be grieved and displeased with anything that happens in the world. It is is direct puss from the nature of the universe; part of which, all particular natures of the world are.

Secondly, when she either is averse from any man, or led by contrary desires or affections, tending to his hurt and prejudice; such as are the souls of them that are angry.

Thirdly, when she is overcome by any pleasure or pain.

Fourthly, when she dissembles, and covertly and falsely either does or says anything.

Fifthly, when she either affects or endeavors anything to no certain end, but rashly and without due reasoning and consideration of how consequential or inconsequential it is to the common end.

For even the least things ought not to be done without relation to the end, and the end of the reasonable creatures is to follow and obey him, who is the reason, as it were, and the law of this great city and ancient commonwealth.

▼

The time of a man's life is as a point. The substance of it is ever flowing, the sense obscure. The whole composition of the body is tending to corruption. His soul is restless, fortune is uncertain, and fame doubtful. It is brief. It is as a stream. So are all things belonging to the body.

As a dream, or as a smoke, so are all that belong to the soul. Our life is a warfare, and a mere pilgrimage. Fame after life is no better than oblivion. What is it then that will adhere and follow? Only one thing, philosophy.

Philosophy consists of this, for a man to preserve that spirit which is within him from all manner of insolence and injuries, and above all pains or pleasures; never to do anything either rashly, or untruthfully, or hypocritically. Wholly to depend on himself and his own proper actions. Contentedly embracing all things that happen to him, as coming from Him from whom he himself also came; and above all things, with all meekness and a calm cheerfulness, to expect death as being nothing else but the resolution of those elements of which every creature is composed.

And if the elements themselves suffer nothing by this, their perpetual conversion of one into another, that dissolution, and alteration which is so common to all, why should it be feared by any? Is not this according to nature? But nothing that is according to nature can be evil, while I was at Carnuntzim.

▲

Chapter Three
On Aging

A man must not only consider how his life wastes and decreases daily, but this also, that if he lives a long time he cannot be certain whether his understanding shall continue as able and sufficient as before for either discreet consideration in matter of businesses or for contemplation. It is the thing where true knowledge of things both divine and human depends.

For once his mind starts to go, his respiration, nutrition, his imaginative, and appetite, and other natural faculties may still continue the same. He shall find no want of them.

But how to make that right use of himself that he should, how to observe exactly in all things that which is right and just? How to redress and rectify all wrong, or sudden apprehensions and imaginations? Even of this particular, to duly consider whether he should live any longer or not. For all such things, wherein the best strength and vigor of the mind require most; his power and ability will be past and gone.

You must therefore know that not only because you are every day nearer to death than others, but also because that intellectual faculty in you, where you are enabled to know the true nature of things, and to order all your actions by that knowledge, daily wastes and decays, or may fail you before you die.

▼

You must also observe that whatever it is that naturally happens to natural things has something in itself that is pleasing and delightful, as a great loaf when it is baked. Some parts of it cleave and part asunder and make the crust of it rugged and unequal, and yet those parts of it, though in some way it is against the art and intention of baking itself, that they are thus cleft and parted, which should have been and were first made all even and uniform, they nevertheless became it, and have a certain peculiar property to stir the appetite.

As figs are accounted fairest and ripest when they begin to shrink and wither, the same with ripe olives, when they are next to putrefaction are they in their proper beauty.

The hanging down of grapes, the brow of a lion, the froth of a foaming wild boar, and many other similar things; though considered by themselves, they are far from any beauty, yet because they happen naturally, they are both comely and delightful. If a man considers all things in the world with a profound mind and apprehension, even among all those things which are but mere accessories and natural appendices, as it were, there will scarcely appear anything to him where he will not find a matter of pleasure and delight.

So he will behold with as much pleasure the true grin of wild beasts, as those which by skillful painters and other artists are imitated. So he will be able to perceive the proper ripeness and beauty of old age, whether in man or woman.

And whatever else it is that is beautiful and alluring in whatever is, with content eyes he will soon find out and discern. Those and many other things will he discern, not credible to everyone, but only to them who are truly and familiarly acquainted, both with nature itself and all natural things.

▼

Having cured many sicknesses, Hippocrates fell sick himself and died. The Chaldeans and Astrologians having foretold the deaths of many, were afterwards themselves surprised by the fates. Alexander and Pompeius, and Caius Caesar, having destroyed so many towns, and cut off in the field so many thousands both of horse and foot soldiers at last were willing to part with their own lives. Heraclitus having written so many natural tracts concerning the last and general conflagration of the world, died afterwards all filled with water within, and all bedaubed with dirt and dung without.

Lice killed Democritus; and Socrates, another sort of

vermin, wicked ungodly men. How then stands the case? You have taken ship, you have sailed, you have come to land, go out if to another life, there also will you find gods, who are everywhere.

If all life and sense shall cease, then will you cease as well to be subject to either pains or pleasures; and to serve and tend this vile cottage; so much the viler, by how much that which ministers to it excels; the one being a rational substance, and a spirit, the other nothing but earth and blood.

▼

Don't spend the remnant of your days in thoughts and fancies concerning other men when it is not in relation to some common good and it hinders you from some other work. That is, don't spend your time in thinking, what such a man does, and to what end. What he says, and what he thinks, and what he is about. Such other things or curiosities, which make a man to rove and wander from the care and observation of that part of himself which is rational and overruling.

See, therefore, in the whole series and connection of your thoughts that you are careful to prevent whatever is idle and impertinent. Especially, whatever is curious and malicious.

You must use yourself to think only of such things, of which if a man upon a sudden should ask you, what it is that you are now thinking, you may answer "This," and "That," freely and boldly that so by your thoughts it may presently appear that you are sincere in all things, and peaceable; as becomes one that is made for society and doesn't regard pleasures, nor gives way to any voluptuous imaginations at all: free from all contentiousness, envy, and suspicion, and from whatever else you would blush to confess your thoughts were set upon.

He that is such is surely someone that does not put off to lay hold on that which is best indeed, a very priest and minister of the gods. Well acquainted and in good correspondence with him, especially, that is seated and placed within himself. As in a temple and obsolete. To whom he also keeps and preserves himself unmarred by pleasure, undaunted by pain; free from any manner of wrong, or harsh language, by himself offered to himself

Not capable of any evil from others, a wrestler of the best sort, and for the highest prize, that he may not be cast down by any passion or affection of his own. Deeply dyed and drenched in righteousness, embracing and accepting with his whole heart whatever either happens or is allotted to him.

One who not often, nor without some great necessity tending to some public good, mindful of what any other, either speaks, or does, or purposes. For those things only that are in his own power, or that are truly his own, are the objects of his employments, and his thoughts are ever taken up with those things which of the whole universe are by the fates or Providence destined and appropriated to himself.

Those things that are his own, and in his own power, he himself takes order, for that they are good. As for those that happen to him, he believes them to be so. For that lot and portion is assigned to everyone, as it is unavoidable and necessary, so is it always profitable.

He remembers besides that whatever partakes of reason is akin to him, and that to care for all men generally is agreeing to the nature of a man. But as for honor and praise, that they ought not generally to be admitted and accepted of from all, but from such only who live according to nature.

As for them that do not, what manner of men they are at home or abroad, day or night, how conditioned they are with what manner of conditions, or with men of what conditions they labor and pass away the time together, he knows and remembers well, and therefore doesn't regard such praise and approbation as proceeding from them who can't like and approve themselves.

▼

Do nothing against your will, nor contrary to the community, nor without due examination, nor reluctantly. Don't try to set out your thoughts with curious neat language.

Be neither a great talker, nor a great undertaker.

Moreover, let your God that is in you rule over you. Find what he has to do with a man; an aged man; a sociable man; a Roman; a prince; one that has ordered his life as one that is expected, as it were, nothing but the sound of the trumpet, sounding a retreat to depart out of this life with all expedition. One who for his word or actions neither needs an oath, nor any man to be a witness.

▼

Be cheerful, and stand in no need, either of other men's help or attendance, or of that rest and tranquility that you must be beholden to others for. Be like one that is straight of himself, or has always been straight, rather than one that has been rectified.

▼

If you find anything in this mortal life better than righteousness, truth, temperance, fortitude, and in general better than a mind contented both with those things which according to right and reason she does, and in those, which without her will and knowledge happen to you by providence, apply yourself to it with your whole heart, and enjoy that which is best freely, wherever you find it.

But if you find nothing to be preferred to that spirit which is within you, if nothing better than to subject you into your own lusts and desires, and not to give way to any fancies or imaginations before you have duly considered them, nothing is better than to withdraw yourself (to use Socrates' words) from all sensuality, and submit yourself to the gods, and to have care of all men in general.

If you will find that all other things in comparison of this are only vile, and of little moment, then don't give way to anything else, which being once though but affected and inclined to, it will no more be in your power without all distraction that you ought to prefer and to pursue after that good, which is your own proper good.

For it is not lawful that anything that is of another and

inferior kind and nature, be it what it will, as either popular applause, or honor, or riches, or pleasures; should be suffered to confront and contest, as it were, with that which is rational, and operationally good. For all these things, if once though but for a while, they begin to please, they presently prevail and pervert a man's mind, or turn a man from the right way.

Therefore, absolutely and freely make choices of that which is best, and stick to it. Now, they say that which is most profitable is best. If they mean profitable to man as he is a rational man, stand to it and maintain it. But if they mean profitable, as he is a creature, only reject it, and from this your tenet and conclusion keep off carefully all plausible shows and colors of external appearance, that you may be able to discern things correctly.

▼

Never esteem anything as profitable which can ever constrain you either to break your faith, to lose your modesty, to hate any man, to suspect, to curse, to dissemble, or to lust after anything that requires the secret of walls or veils. But whoever prefers his rational part and spirit before all things, and the sacred mysteries of virtue which issue from it, he shall never lament and exclaim, never sigh. He will never want either solitude or company. Which is chiefest of all, he shall live without either desire or fear.

And as for life, whether for a long or short time he shall enjoy his soul thus compassed about with a body, he is altogether indifferent. For if even now he were to depart, he is as ready for it, as for any other action, which may be performed with modesty and decency. For all his life long, his only care is that his mind may always be occupied in such intentions and objects as are proper to a rational, sociable creature.

▼

In the mind that is truly disciplined and purged, you can't find anything either foul or impure, or as if it was festered. There is nothing that is either servile or affected, no partial tie, no malicious aversion, nothing obnoxious, nothing concealed. Death can never surprise the life of such a one as imperfect, as of an actor that should die before he had ended, or the play itself were at an end, a man might speak.

▼

Use your opinion making faculty with all honor and respect, for in her is indeed all, that your opinions don't cause anything in your understanding to be contrary to either nature, or the proper constitution of a rational creature.

The end and object of a rational constitution is to do nothing rashly, to be kindly affected towards men, and in all things willingly to submit to the gods. Therefore, casting all other things aside, keep yourself to these few and always remember that no man can be said properly to live in more than that which is now present, which is but a moment of time.

Whatever is besides either is already past, or uncertain. The time therefore that any man lives is but a little, and the place where he lives is but a very little corner of the earth. The greatest fame that can remain of a man after his death, even that is but little, and that too, such as it is while it is, is by the succession of silly mortal men preserved, who likewise shall shortly die, and even while they live don't know what in very deed they themselves are, and much less can know one who long before is dead and gone.

▼

To these ever-present helps and mementos, let one more be added, ever to make a particular description and delineation of every object that presents itself to your mind, that you may fully and thoroughly contemplate it in its own proper nature, bare and naked.

Contemplate it wholly, and severally, divided into its several parts and quarters, and then in your mind, to call both it, and those things of which it consists, and in which it shall be resolved by their own proper, true names and appellations.

For there is nothing so effectual to cause true

magnanimity as to be able truly and methodically to examine and consider all things that happen in this life. To penetrate into their natures, that at the same time, this also may concur in our apprehensions: what is the true use of it?

And what is the true nature of this universe, to which it is useful? How much in regard of the universe may it be esteemed? How much in regard of man, a citizen of the supreme city, of which all other cities in the world are as it were but houses and families?

▼

What is this that my fancy is now set upon? Of what things does it consist? How long can it last? Which of all the virtues is the proper virtue for this present use? As whether meekness, fortitude, truth, faith, sincerity, contentment, or any of the rest?

Of everything therefore you must use yourself to say, This immediately comes from God, this by that fatal connection, and concatenation of things, or (which almost comes to one) by some coincidental casualty. And as for this, it proceeds from my neighbor, my kinsman, my fellow. It proceeds through his ignorance indeed, because he doesn't know what is truly natural to him; but I know, and therefore carry myself towards him according to the natural law of fellowship; that is, kindly, and justly.

As for those things that of themselves are altogether indifferent, as in my best judgment I conceive everything to deserve more or less, so I carry myself towards it.

▼

If you will intend that which is present, following the rule of right and reason carefully, solidly, meekly, and will not intermix any other businesses, but shall study this only to preserve your spirit unpolluted, and pure, and shall cleave to him without either hope or fear of anything, in all things that you will either do or speak, contenting yourself with heroic truth, you will live happily. From this, there is no man that can hinder you.

30

▼

As physicians and surgeons always have their instruments ready at hand for all sudden cures, so you always have your dogma in a readiness for the knowledge of things both divine and human. Whatever you do, even in the smallest things that you do, you must always remember that mutual relation and connection that is between these two divine things and human things. For without relation to God, you will never speed in any worldly actions; nor on the other side in any divinity, without some respect given to human things.

▼

Don't be deceived; you will never live to read your moral commentaries, nor the acts of the famous Romans and Grecians; nor those excerpts from several books, all of which you had provided and laid up for yourself against your old age, having, therefore, an end, and giving over all vain hopes, help yourself in time if you care for yourself, as you ought to do.

▼

To steal, to sow, to buy, to be at rest, to see what is to be done (which is not seen by the eyes, but by another kind of sight) what these words mean, and how many ways to be understood, they do not understand. The body, the soul, the understanding. As the senses naturally belong to the body, and the desires and affections to the soul, so does dogma to understanding.

▼

To be capable of fancies and imaginations is common to man and beast. To be violently drawn and moved by the lusts and desires of the soul is proper to wild beasts and monsters, such as Phalaris and Nero were.

To follow reason for ordinary duties and actions is common to them also, who don't believe that there are any gods, and for their advantage would not hesitate to betray their own country, and who, when the doors once are shut on them, dare to do anything.

If therefore all other things are common to these as

well, it follows that for a man to like and embrace all things that happen and are destined to him, and not to trouble and molest that spirit which is seated in the temple of his own breast, with a multitude of vain fancies and imaginations, but to keep him benevolent and to obey him as a god, never either speaking anything contrary to truth, or doing anything contrary to justice, is the only true property of a good man.

And such a one, though no man should believe that he lives as he does, either sincerely and consciously, or cheerful and contentedly. Yet is he neither with any man at all angry for it, nor diverted by it from the way that leads to the end of his life, through which a man must pass pure, ever ready to depart, and willing of himself without any compulsion to fit and accommodate himself to his proper lot and portion.

▲

Chapter Four
The Pale Blue Dot

That inward mistress part of a man, if it is in its own true natural temper, is towards all worldly chances and events ever so disposed and affected that it will easily turn and apply itself to that which may be. It is within its own power to encompass when that can't be what it was intended to be at first.

For it never does absolutely apply itself fully to any one object, but whatever it is that it now intends and prosecutes, it prosecutes it with exception and reservation. It is what it is that falls contrary to its first intentions, even though it makes its proper object afterwards.

Even as the fire, when it prevails upon those things that are in its way, by which things indeed a little fire would have been quenched, but a great fire soon turns to its own nature, and so consume whatever comes in its way. Yes, by those very things it is made greater and greater.

▼

Let nothing be done rashly, and at random, but all things according to the most exact and perfect rules of the art.

▼

They seek private retiring places for themselves, as country villages, the sea-shore, mountains. Yes, you yourself long after such places. But all this you must know proceeds from simplicity in the highest degree. At what time you wish, it is in your power to retire into yourself, and to be at rest, and free from all businesses.

A man cannot retire anywhere better than to his own soul; especially he who is beforehand provided of such things within, which whenever he does withdraw himself to look in, may presently afford him perfect ease and tranquility. By tranquility I understand a decent orderly disposition and carriage, free from all confusion and tumult.

Then afford yourself this retiring continually, and

33

thereby refresh and renew yourself. Let these precepts be brief and fundamental, which as soon as you call them to mind, may suffice to purge your soul thoroughly, and to send you away well pleased with those things, whatever they are, which now again after this short withdrawing of your soul into herself you then return to.

For what is it that you are offended by? Can it be the wickedness of men, when you call to mind this conclusion, that all reasonable creatures are made for one another? And that it is part of justice to bear with them? And that it is against their wills that they offend?

And how many already, who once likewise prosecuted their enmities, suspected, hated, and fiercely contended, are now long ago stretched out, and reduced to ashes? It is time for you to make an end.

As for those things which among the common chances of the world happen to you as your particular lot and portion, can you be displeased with any of them, when you call that our ordinary dilemma to mind, either a providence, or Democritus his atoms? And with it, whatever we brought to prove that the whole world is as it were one city?

And as for your body, what can you fear, if you consider that your mind and understanding, when once it has recollected itself, and knows its own power, has in this life and breath (whether it runs smoothly and gently, or harshly and rudely), no interest at all, but is altogether indifferent? And whatever else you have heard and assented to concerning either pain or pleasure?

But the care of your honor and reputation might distract you? How can that be, if you look back and consider both how quickly all things that are, are forgotten, and what an immense chaos of eternity was before, and will follow after all things: and the vanity of praise, and the inconstancy and variability of human judgments and opinions, and the narrowness of the place where it is limited and circumscribed?

For the whole earth is but as one point; and of it, this

inhabited part of it, is but a very little part; and of this part, how many in number, and what manner of men are they, that will commend you? What remains then, but that you often put in practice this kind of retiring of yourself, to this little part of yourself; and above all things, keep yourself from distraction, and don't intend anything vehemently, but be free and consider all things, as a man whose proper object is Virtue, as a man whose true nature is to be kind and sociable, as a citizen, as a mortal creature.

Among other things to consider and look into you must use to withdraw yourself, let these two be among the most obvious and at hand: one, that the things or objects themselves don't reach to the soul, but stand outside, still and quiet, and that it is from the opinion only which is within that all the tumult and all the trouble proceeds.

The next, that all these things, which you now see, shall within a very little while be changed, and be no more. Ever call to mind how many changes and alterations in the world you yourself have already been an eyewitness of in your time. This world is mere change, and this life, opinion.

▼

If to understand and to be reasonable is normal for all men, then reason, for which we are termed reasonable, is normal for everyone. If reason is general, then reason is also that which prescribes what is to be done and what not, is common to all.

If that is, then it is natural law. If it is law, then we are fellow-citizens. If so, then are we partners in some commonwealth. If so, then the world is as if it were a city. For which other commonwealth is it, that all men can be said to be members of?

From this common city it is that understanding, reason, and law is derived to us, for from where else? For as that which in me is earthly I have from some common earth; and that which is moist from some other element is imparted; as my breath and life has its proper fountain; and that likewise which is dry and fiery in me.

For there is nothing which does not proceed from something; as also there is nothing that can be reduced to mere nothing, so also is there some common beginning from where my understanding has proceeded.

▼

As birth is, so is death. They are secrets of nature's wisdom: a mixture of elements, resolved into the same elements again, a thing which surely no man ought to be ashamed of. In a series of other fatal events and consequences, which a rational creature is subject to, not improper or incongruous, nor contrary to the natural and proper constitution of man himself.

▼

Such and such things, from such and such causes, must of necessity proceed. He who would not have such things to happen is as he who would have the fig-tree grow without any sap or moisture. In sum, remember this, that within a very little while, both you and he shall both be dead, and after a little while more, not so much as your names and memories shall be remaining.

▼

Let opinion be taken away, and no man will think himself wronged. If no man thinks himself wronged, then there is no more any such thing as wrong. That which doesn't make man worse, can't make his life worse, neither can it hurt him either inwardly or outwardly. It was expedient in nature that it should be so, and therefore necessary.

▼

Whatever happens in the world happens justly, and so if you will take heed, you will find it. I say not only is it in the right order by a series of inevitable consequences, but according to justice and, as it were, by way of equal distribution, according to the true worth of everything.

Continue, then, to take notice of it, as you have begun, and whatever you do, don't do it without this proviso, that it is a thing of that nature that a good man (as the word good is properly taken) may do it. Observe this carefully in every action.

▼

Imagine no such things that someone who has wronged you would imagine, or would have you to imagine, but look into the matter itself and see what it truly is.

▼

You must always have these two rules in a readiness: First, do nothing at all except what reason suggests to you, proceeding that from that regal and supreme part shall be for the good and benefit of men.

And secondly, if any man that is present can correct you or to turn you from some erroneous persuasion, that you always be ready to change your mind, and this change to proceed not from any respect of any pleasure or credit depending thereon, but always from some probable apparent ground of justice, or of some public good thereby to be furthered; or from some other such inducement.

▼

Do you have reason? I have. Then why don't you make use of it? For if your reason does its part, what more can you require?

▼

As a part hereto you have had a particular subsistence, and now will you vanish away into the common substance of Him, who first created you, or rather you will be resumed again into that original rational substance, out of which all others have issued, and are propagated. Many small pieces of frankincense are set upon the same altar, one drops first and is consumed, another after; and it comes all to one.

▼

Within ten days, if it happens, you will be esteemed a god by them, who now if you will return to the dogma and to the honoring of reason, will esteem you as no better than a mere brute, and of an ape.

▼

It isn't as though you had thousands of years to live. Death hangs over you. While you still live, while you can, be good.

▼

Now, he gains much time and leisure who is not curious to know what his neighbor has said, or has done, or has attempted, but only what he does himself, that it may be just and holy? Or to express it in Agathos' words, "Not to look about upon the evil conditions of others, but to run on straight in the line, without any loose and extravagant agitation."

▼

Whoever is greedy for credit and reputation after his death does not consider that they by whom he is remembered shall soon after every one of them be dead; and they likewise that succeed those; until at last all memory, which hereto by the succession of men admiring and soon after dying has had its course will be quite extinct.

But suppose that both they that shall remember you, and your memory with them should be immortal, what is that to you? I will not say to you after you're dead; but even to your living, what is your praise? But only for a secret and politic consideration, which we call economics or dispensation.

For as for that, that it is the gift of nature, whatever is commended in you, what might be objected from there, let that be omitted as unseasonable, now that we are upon another consideration. That which is fair and good, whatever it is, and in what respect it is that it is fair and good, it is so of itself, and terminates in itself, not admitting praise as a part or member.

That which is praised, therefore, is not thereby made either better or worse. This I understand even of those things that are commonly called fair and good, as those which are commended either for the matter itself, or for curious workmanship.

As for that which is truly good, what can it stand in

need of more than either justice or truth, or more than either kindness and modesty? Which of all those, either becomes good or fair, because commended? Does being despised cause any damage? does the emerald become worse in itself, or more vile if it be not commended? does gold, or ivory, or purple? Is there anything that does, though never so common, as a knife, a flower, or a tree?

▼

"If it's so that the souls remain after death," say they that will not believe it, "how is the air from all eternity able to contain them?"

"How is the earth." say I, "ever from that time able to Contain the bodies of them that are buried?" For as here the change and resolution of dead bodies into another kind of subsistence (whatever it is) makes place for other dead bodies, so the souls after death transferred into the air, after they have conversed there a while, are either by way of transmutation, or transfusion, or conflagration, received again into that original rational substance, from which all others proceed, and so give way to those souls who before were coupled and associated with bodies, now begin to subsist singly.

This, upon a supposition that the souls after death subsist single for a while, may be answered. And here, (besides the number of bodies, so buried and contained by the earth), we may further consider the number of several beasts, eaten by us men, and by other creatures. For notwithstanding that such a multitude of them is daily consumed, and as it were buried in the bodies of the eaters, yet is the same place and body able to contain them, by reason of their conversion, partly into blood, and partly into air and fire.

What in these things is the speculation of truth? To divide things into that which is passive and material; and that which is active and formal.

▼

Not to wander out of the way on every motion and

desire; to perform that which is just; and ever to be careful to attain to the true natural apprehension of every fancy that presents itself.

▼

Whatever is expedient to the world is expedient to me; nothing can either be unseasonable to me, or out of date, which to the world is seasonable. Whatever its seasons bear, shall always be esteemed by me as happy fruit, and increase. Oh, Nature! from you are all things, in you all things subsist, and all tend to you. Could he say of Athens, you lovely city of Cecrops[8]; and will not you say of the world, you lovely city of God?

Cecrops (Calenbild in Palermo).

▼

They will often say "Don't meddle with too many things if you want to live cheerfully." Certainly there is nothing better than for a man to confine himself to necessary actions, to such and so many only, as reason in a creature that knows itself born for society will command and join.

This will not only obtain that cheerfulness which is from goodness, but also that which usually proceeds from a paucity of actions. For since it is so that most of those things which we either speak or do are unnecessary. If a man cuts them off, it must follow that he will thereby gain a lot of leisure, and save much trouble, and therefore at every action a man must privately, by way of admonition, suggest to himself, "What? Now that I go about, May this not be of the number of unnecessary actions?"

Neither must he not only cut off actions, but unnecessary thoughts and imaginations as well, so that unnecessary consequent actions will be better prevented and cut off.

▼

Think also how a good man's life, a life of one who is well pleased with those things whatever, which among the

40

normal changes and chances of this world fall to his own lot and share, and can live well contented and fully satisfied in the justice of his own proper present action, and in the goodness of his disposition for the future will agree with you.

You have had experience of that other kind of life, now try this as well. Don't trouble yourself any more, reduce yourself to perfect simplicity. Does any man offend? It is against himself that he offends. Why should it trouble you? has anything happened to you?

It is well, whatever it is, that which of all the common chances of the world from the very beginning in the series of all other things that have happened or will happen, was destined and appointed to you.

To comprehend it all in a few words, our life is short; we must endeavor to gain the present time with best discretion and justice. Use recreation with sobriety.

▼

Either this world is a cosmos or comely piece, because all are disposed and governed by certain order, or if it is a mixture, though confused, yet still it is a comely piece. For it's possible that in you there should be any beauty at all, and that in the whole world there should be nothing but disorder and confusion? And all things in it too, by natural different properties one from another differentiated and distinguished; and yet all through diffused, and by natural sympathy, one to another united, as they are?

▼

A black or malign disposition, an effeminate disposition; a hard inexorable disposition, a wild inhuman disposition, a sheepish disposition, a childish disposition; a stupid, a false, a scurrilous, a fraudulent, a tyrannical—what then? If he is a stranger in the world that doesn't know the things that are in it, why is he not be a stranger as well that wonders at the things that are done in it?

▼

He who flees from reason is truly a fugitive from

society. He who cannot see with the eyes of his understanding is blind. He is poor who needs another, and does not have in himself all of the things needful for this life. He a pimple of the world, who by being discontented with those things that happen to him in the world, as it were abandons the world, and separates himself from common nature's rational administration.

For the same nature it is that brings this to you whatever it is that first brought you into the world. He raises sedition in the city, who by irrational actions withdraws his own soul from that one and common soul of all rational creatures.

▼

There is one who without so much as a coat; and there is one who is without so much as a book, puts philosophy in practice. "I am half naked, neither have I bread to eat, and yet I don't depart from reason," says one. But I say; I want the food of good teaching, and instructions, and yet I don't depart from reason.

▼

Whatever art and profession you have learned, endeavor to affect it, and comfort yourself in it, and pass the remainder of your life as one who commits himself with his whole heart and whatever belongs to him to the gods. As for men, don't carry yourself either tyrannically or submissively towards any.

▼

Consider in my mind, for example's sake, the times of Vespasian:[8] you will only see the same things; some marrying, some bringing up children, some sick, some dying, some fighting, some feasting, some selling, some tilling, some flattering, some boasting, some suspecting, some undermining, some wishing to die, some fretting and murmuring at their present state, some wooing, some hoarding, some seeking to be mayor, and some after kingdoms. And isn't their age quite over, and ended?

Again, consider now the times of Trajan.[9] There likewise you see the very same things, and that age also is now over and ended. In the like manner consider other periods, both of times and of whole nations, and see how many men, after they had with all their might and main intended and prosecuted some one worldly thing or other soon after dropped away, and were resolved into the elements.

But especially you must call to mind them, whom you yourself in your lifetime have known much distracted about silly things, and in the meantime neglecting to do that, and closely and inseparably (as fully satisfied with it) to adhere to it, which their own proper constitution required. And here you must remember that your carriage in every business must be according to the worth and due proportion of it, for so will you not easily be tired out and vexed, if you will not dwell upon small matters longer than is fitting.

▼

Those words which once were common and ordinary have now become obscure and obsolete; and so the names of men once commonly known and famous have now become in a manner obscure and obsolete names. Camillus, Cieso, Volesius, Leonnatus; not long after, Scipio, Cato, then Augustus, then Adrianus, then Antoninus Pius. All these in a short time will be out of date, and, as things of another world as it were, become fabulous.

And this I say of them who once shined as the wonders of their ages, for as for the rest, no sooner are they expired than with them all their fame and memory. And what is it then that shall always be remembered? All is vanity.

What is it that we must bestow our care and diligence on? Even on this only: that our minds and wills be just, that our actions be charitable, that our speech never be deceitful, or that our understanding not be subject to error. That our inclination be always set to embrace whatever shall happen to us, as necessary, as usual, as ordinary, as flowing from such a beginning, and such a fountain from which both you yourself and all things are.

Willingly therefore, and wholly surrender to that fatal concatenation, yielding up yourself to the fates, to be disposed of at their pleasure.

▼

Whatever is now present, and from day to day has its existence; all objects of memories, and the minds and memories themselves, incessantly consider that all things that are, have their being by change and alteration.

Therefore use yourself often to meditate upon this, that the nature of the universe delights in nothing more than in altering those things that are, and in making others like them. So that we may say, that whatever is, is only as it was the seed of that which shall be. For if you think that that there is only seed, which either the earth or the womb receives, you're very simple.

▼

You're now ready to die, and yet you haven't attained that perfect simplicity: you are still subject to many troubles and perturbations; not yet free from all fear and suspicion of external accidents; nor yet either so meekly disposed towards all men, as you should be; or so affected as one, whose only study and only wisdom is to be just in all his actions.

▼

Behold and observe what the state of their rational part is, and those that the world accounts wise, see what things they flee from and are afraid of; and what things they hunt.

▼

Your evil can't live In another man's mind and understanding, nor in any proper temper or distemper of the natural constitution of your body, which is but as it were the coat or cottage of your soul. Where then, can the conceit and apprehension of any misery subsist but in that part of you?

Don't let that part admit any such conceit, and then all is well. Though your body which is so near it should either be cut or burned, or suffer any corruption or putrefaction, yet let that part to which it belongs to judge of these, will be at rest. That is, let her judge this, that whatever it is that equally may happen to a wicked man and to a good man is neither good nor evil.

For that which happens equally to him that lives according to nature, and to him that does not, is neither according to nature, nor against it; and consequentially neither good nor bad.

▼

Always consider and think of the world as being but one living substance, and having but one soul, and how all things in the world are terminated into one sensitive power, and are done by one general motion, as it were, and deliberation of that one soul, and how all things that are, concur in the cause of one another's being, and by what manner of connection and concatenation all things happen.

▼

That better and divine part excepted, what are you but as Epictetus said well—a wretched soul, appointed to carry a carcass up and down?

▼

To suffer change can cause no harm, as it is not beneficial, by change to attain to being. The age and time of the world is as it were a flood and swift current, consisting of the things that are brought to pass in the world. For as soon as anything has appeared, and is passed away, another succeeds, and that also will presently be out of sight.

▼

In the course of nature, whatever happens in the world is as usual and ordinary as a rose in the spring, and fruit in summer. Of the same nature is sickness and death; slander, and lying in wait, and whatever else fools use to cause either joy or sorrow. That, whatever it is that comes after, always does so very naturally, and as it were familiarly, follow upon that which was before.

For you must consider the things of the world, not as a

45

loose independent number, consisting merely of necessary events, but as a discreet connection of things orderly and harmoniously disposed. There is then to be seen in the things of the world, not a bare succession, but an admirable correspondence and affinity.

▼

Never let what Heraclitus[10] said leave your mind: that the death of earth is water, and the death of water is air, and the death of air is fire, and so on. Also remember who was ignorant where the way led, and how reason being the thing by which all things in the world are administered, and which men are continually and most inwardly conversant with.

Yet is the thing, which ordinarily they are most in opposition to, and how those things which daily happen among them don't cease to be strange to them daily.

We should not either speak or do anything as men do in their sleep, by opinion and bare imagination, or then we think we speak and do, and that we must not be as children, who follow their father's example; for best reason alleging their bare successive tradition from our forefathers we have received it.

▼

If any of the gods would tell you that you will certainly die tomorrow or the next day, unless you were extremely base and cowardly you would not take it as a great benefit to die the day after tomorrow rather to die the next day. For alas, what is the difference? So, for the same reason, think it no great matter to die rather many years after than the very next day.

▼

Let it be your perpetual meditation about how many physicians who once looked so grim, and so theatrically shrunk their brows upon their patients, are dead and gone themselves. How many astrologers, after that in great ostentation had foretold the death of some others. How many philosophers after so many elaborate tracts and volumes concerning either mortality or immortality.

46

How many brave captains and commanders, after the death and slaughter of so many. How many kings and tyrants, after they had with such horror and insolence abused their power over men's lives, as though they had themselves been immortal. How many, that I may so speak, whole cities, both men and towns: Helice, Pompeii, Herculaneum, and others innumerable are dead and gone.

Run them over also, whom you yourself, one after another, have known in your time to drop away. Such and such a one took care of such and such a one's burial, and soon after was buried himself. So one, so another. All things in a short time.

For herein lies all indeed, ever to look upon all worldly things as things for their continuance, that are but for a day. For their worth, most vile, and contemptible, as for example, what is man? That which but the other day when he was conceived was vile snot; and within few days shall be either an embalmed carcass, or mere ashes.

Thus must you according to truth and nature, thoroughly consider how man's life is but for a very moment of time, and so depart meekly and contented, even as if a ripe olive falling should praise the ground that bare her, and give thanks to the tree that begat her.

▼

You must be like a promontory of the sea, though against which the waves beat continually it itself stands, and about it are those swelling waves stilled and quieted.

▼

Oh, wretched me, to whom this mischance is happened! No, happy me, to whom this thing being happened, I can continue without grief; neither wounded by that which is present, nor in fear of that which is to come.

For as for this, it might have happened to any man, but any man having such a thing befall him could not have continued without grief. Why then should that rather be an unhappiness, than this a happiness? But however, can you, Oh man, turn that unhappiness, which is no mischance to the nature of man.

Can you think that a mischance to the nature of man, which is not contrary to the end and will of his nature? Then what you have learned is the will of man's nature? Then does that which has happened to you hinder you from being just? Or magnanimous? Or temperate? Or wise? Or circumspect? Or true? Or modest? Or free? Or from anything else of all those things in the present, enjoying and possession of the nature of man (as then enjoying all that is proper to her), is fully satisfied?

Now to conclude; upon all occasion of sorrow, remember from now on to make use of this dogma, that whatever it is that has happened to you is indeed no such thing of itself, as a misfortune; but that to bear it generously, is certainly great happiness.

▼

It is only an ordinary coarse remedy, yet it is a good effective one against the fear of death for a man to consider in his mind the examples of such, who greedily and covetously (as it were) for a long time enjoyed their lives. What have they got more than those whose deaths have been untimely? Are not they themselves dead at the last?

As Cadiciant's, Fabius, Julianus Lepidus, or any other who in their lifetime having buried many, were at last buried themselves. The whole space of any man's life is but little; and as little as it is, with what troubles, with what manner of dispositions, and in the society of how wretched a body must it be passed!

Then let it be to you altogether as a matter of indifference. For if you will look backward; behold, what an infinite chaos of time does present itself to you. As infinite a chaos, if you will look forward. In that which is so infinite, what difference can there be between that which lives but three days, and that which lives three ages?

▼

Let your course ever be the most comprehensive way. The most comprehensive is that which is according to nature. That is, in all both words and deeds, ever to follow that which is most sound and perfect. For such a resolution will free a man from all trouble, strife, dissembling, and ostentation.

▲

Chapter Five
Pain and Pleasure

In the morning when you find yourself unwilling to rise, consider that it is to go about a man's work that I have awakened. Am I then still unwilling to go about that which I myself was born and brought forth into this world for?

Or was I made for this, to lay me down, and make much of myself in a warm bed? "Oh, but this is pleasing." And was it then for this that you were born, that you might enjoy pleasure? Was it not in very truth for this, that you might always be busy and in action?

Don't you see how all things in the world besides, how every tree and plant, sparrows and ants, spiders and bees, how all in their kind are intent, as it were, to perform in an orderly manner whatever (towards the preservation of this orderly universe) naturally becomes and belongs to them? And will you not do that which a man should do? Will you not run to do that which your nature requires?

"But you must have some rest." Yes, you must. Nature has of that also, as well as eating and drinking, allowed you a certain stint. But you go beyond your stint, and beyond that which would suffice, and in a matter of action, there you come short of that which you may. It must be, therefore, that you don't love yourself, for if you did, you would also love your nature, and that which your nature does propose to herself as her end.

Others, as many as take pleasure in their trade and profession, can even pine themselves at their works, and neglect their bodies and their food for it. Do you honor your nature less than an ordinary mechanic his trade, or a good dancer his? Than a covetous man his silver, and vainglorious man applause? These to whatever they take an affection, can be content to want their meat and sleep, to further that every one which he affects. Shall actions tending to the common good of human society, seem more vile to you, or a warrior of less respect and intention?

▼

How easy a thing is it for a man to put off from him all turbulent adventitious imaginations, and presently to be in perfect rest and tranquility!

▼

Think of yourself as one who is fit to speak or do anything that is according to nature, and don't let the reproach or report of some that may ensue upon it ever deter you. If it's right and honest to be spoken or done, don't undervalue yourself so much as to be discouraged from it.

As for them, they have their own rational over-ruling part, and their own proper inclination which you must not stand and look about to take notice of, but go on straight, where both your own particulars, and the common nature lead you. The way of both these is but one.

▼

I will continue my course of actions according to nature until I fall and cease, breathing out my last breath into the air that I continually breathed in when I lived. Falling on that earth, out of whose gifts and fruits my father gathered his seed, my mother her blood, and my nurse her milk, out of which for so many years I have been provided, with both food and drink. And lastly, which bears me who had tread upon it, and bore me while in so many ways I abuse it, or so freely make use of it, so many ways to so many ends.

▼

No man could admire you for your sharp, acute language, such is your natural disability that way. Be it so, yet there are many other good things for the want of which you can't plead the lack or natural ability. Let those who depend wholly on you be seen: sincerity, gravity, laboriousness, contempt of pleasures, not querulousness, content with little, kind, free, avoiding all superfluity, avoiding all vain prattling, magnanimity.

Don't you see how many things there are which

notwithstanding any pretense of natural indisposition and unfitness you might have performed and exhibited, yet still you voluntarily continue drooping downwards? Or will you say that it is through defect of your natural constitution that you are constrained to murmur, to be base and wretched to flatter? Now to accuse, and now to please, and pacify your body, to be vainglorious, to be so giddy-headed, and unsettled in your thoughts?

No (the gods witnesses) of all these you might have gotten rid of long ago. Only, this you must have been contented with, to have borne the blame of one that is somewhat slow and dull, wherein you must exercise yourself as one who neither takes his natural defect much to heart, nor yet pleased himself in it.

▼

There are such who, when they have done a good turn to any are ready to make them pay for it, and to require retaliation. There are others who, though they don't stand on retaliation to require any, still think of themselves nevertheless that such a one is their debtor, and they know as their word is what they have done. There are yet others who, when they have done any such thing, do not so much as know what they have done; but are like to the vine, which bears her grapes, and when once she has borne her own proper fruit, is contented and seeks for no further recompense.

As a horse after a race, and a hunting dog when he has hunted, and a bee when she has made her honey don't look for applause and commendation; so neither does that man who correctly understands his own nature when he has done a good turn—but from one proceeded to do another, even as the vine after she has once borne fruit in her own proper season, is ready for another time.

You therefore must be one of them, who what they do, barely do it without any further thought, and are in a manner insensible of what they do. "No, but," will some reply, "a rational man is bound to this very thing, to understand what it is that he does." For it is the property, say they, of one that is naturally sociable to be sensible, that he operates sociably; nay, and to desire, that the part of himself that is sociably dealt with, should be sensible of it too. I answer, "That which you say is true indeed, but the true meaning of that which is said, you do not understand. And therefore you are one of those first, whom I mentioned. For they also are led by a probable appearance of reason. But if you desire to truly understand what it is that is said, don't fear that you will therefore give over any sociable action."

▼

The form of the Athenians' prayer went like this: "O rain, rain, good Jupiter, upon all the grounds and fields that belong to the Athenians." Either we should not pray at all, or absolutely and freely; and not every one for himself in particular alone.

▼

As we often say, the physician has prescribed riding to this man and cold baths to another; to a third, to go barefoot. So it is the same to say, the nature of the universe has prescribed to this man sickness, or blindness, or some loss, or damage or some such thing.

For as there, when we say of a physician that he has prescribed anything, our meaning is that he has appointed this for that, as subordinate and conducing to health: so here, whatever happens to anyone, is ordained to him as a thing subordinate to the fates. Therefore we say of such things, that they happen, or fall together, as of square stones, when either in walls, or pyramids in a certain position they fit one another, and agree as it were in harmony. The masons say that they come together as if you would say, fall together. So that in general, though the things are different that make it, the consent or harmony itself is but one.

And as the whole world is made up of all the particular bodies of the world, one perfect and complete body, of the same nature that particular bodies, so is the destiny of particular causes and events one general one, of the same nature that particular causes are. What I now say, even they that are mere idiots are not ignorant of, for they often say *touto eferen autw;* that is, his destiny has brought this upon him.

Therefore, this is properly by the fates and particularly brought upon this, as that to this in particular is prescribed by the physician. Therefore let us accept these in like manner, as we do those that are prescribed to us by our physicians. We shall find them to contain many harsh things for them also in themselves; but we nevertheless, in hope of health, and recovery, accept them.

Let the fulfilling and accomplishment of those things which the common nature has determined be to you as your health. Accept then, and be pleased with whatever happens, though otherwise harsh and unpleasant, as tending to that end, to the health and welfare of the universe, and to Jove's happiness and prosperity. For this, whatever it may be, would not have been produced had it not been for the good of the universe.

For neither does any ordinary particular nature bring anything to pass that is not to whatever is within the sphere of its own proper administration and government, agreeable and subordinate. For these two considerations, then, you must be well pleased with anything that happens to you. First, because it was brought to pass for you, properly, and to you it was prescribed, and that from the very beginning by the series and connection of the first causes, it has ever had a reference to you.

And secondly, because the good success and perfect welfare, and indeed the very continuance of Him, that is the Administrator of the whole, does in a manner depend on it. For the whole (because whole, therefore entire and perfect) is maimed, and mutilated, if you will cut off anything at all, whereby the coherence, and contiguity as of parts, so of causes, is maintained and preserved. Certainly it is, that you (as much as lies in you) cut off, and in some sort violently take something away, as often as you are displeased with anything that happens.

▼

Don't be discontented or disheartened or out of hope if it often doesn't succeed so well, even with you punctually and precisely doing everything according to the right dogma, but being once cast off, return to them again. As for those many and more frequent occurrences, either of worldly distractions or human infirmities which as a man you can't but in some measure be subjected to, don't be discontented with them.

But however, love and affect that only which you should return to: a philosopher's life, and proper occupation after the most exact manner. And when you return to your philosophy, don't return to it as the manner of some, after play and liberty as it were, to their schoolmasters and pedagogues; but as they that have sore eyes to their sponge and egg, or as another to his poultice, or as others to their pain cream. So it will not make it a matter of ostentation at all to obey reason, but of ease and comfort.

And remember that philosophy requires nothing of you but what your nature requires, and would you yourself desire anything that is not according to nature? For which of these do you say, that which is according to nature or against it, it is of itself more kind and pleasing? Is it not especially for that respect that pleasure itself is to so many men's harm and overthrow most prevalent, because they are often esteemed most kind and natural? But consider well whether magnanimity rather, and true liberty, and true simplicity, and equanimity, and holiness; whether these aren't most kind and natural?

And prudence itself, what more kind and amiable than it, when you will truly consider with yourself what it is through all the proper objects of your rational intellectual faculty currently to go on without any fall or stumble? As for the things of the world, their true nature is in a manner so involved with obscurity, that to many philosophers, and those no mean ones, they seemed altogether incomprehensible, and the Stoics themselves, though they judge them not altogether incomprehensible, yet scarce and not without much difficulty, comprehensible, so that all assent of ours is fallible, for who is he that is infallible in his conclusions?

From the nature of things, pass now to their subjects and matter. How temporary, how vile are they such as I may be in the power and possession of some abominable loose liver, of some common strumpet, of some notorious oppressor and extortioner. Pass from there to the dispositions of them that you ordinarily converse with, how hardly do we bear, even with the most loving and amiable!

That I may not say, how hard it is for us to bear even with our own selves, in such obscurity, and impurity of things, in such and so continual a flux both of the substances and time, both of the motions themselves, and things moved. What it is that we can fasten upon, either to honor and respect especially, or seriously, and studiously to seek after, I cannot so much as conceive. For indeed they are contrary things.

▼

You must comfort yourself in the expectation of your natural dissolution, and in the meantime not grieve at the delay, but rest contented in these two things.

First, that nothing will happen to you which is not according to the nature of the universe. Second, that it is in your power to do nothing against your own proper God and inward spirit. For it is not in any man's power to constrain you to transgress against him.

▼

What use do I make of my soul? From time to time and upon all occasions you must put this question to yourself. What is now that part of me which they call the rational mistress part employed with? Whose soul do I now properly possess? A child's? Or a youth's? A woman's? Or a tyrant's? Some brute, or some wild beast's soul?

What those things themselves which by the greatest part are esteemed good are, you may gather even from this: for if a man shall hear things mentioned as good, which are really good indeed, such as prudence, temperance, justice, fortitude, after so much is heard and conceived, he cannot endure to hear of any more, for the word "good" is properly spoken of them.

But as for those which are esteemed good by the vulgar, if he shall hear them mentioned as good, he hearkens for more. He is well contented to hear that what is spoken by the comedian, is but familiarly and popularly spoken, so that even the vulgar apprehend the difference.

For why is it else that this doesn't offend and doesn't need to be excused, when virtues are styled good, but that which is spoken in commendation of wealth, pleasure, or honor, we entertain it only as merrily and pleasantly spoken? Proceed therefore, and inquire further, whether it may not be that those things also which being mentioned upon the stage were merrily, and with great applause of the multitude, scoffed at with this jest that they that possessed them had not in all the world of their own, (such was their affluence and plenty) so much as a place where to void their excrement.

Whether, I say, those ought not also in very deed to be much respected, and esteemed of, as the only things that are truly good.

▼

All that I consist of is either form or matter. No corruption can reduce either of these to nothing, for neither did I become a subsistent creature from nothing. Every part of me then will by mutation be disposed into a certain part of the whole world, and that in time into another part. And so in infinity by which kind of mutation I also became what I am, and so did they that begot me, and they before them, and so upwards in infinity.

For so we may be allowed to speak, though the age and

government of the world are to some certain periods of time limited and confined.

▼

Reason and rational power are faculties which content themselves with themselves and their own proper operations. And as for their first inclination and motion, they take that from themselves. But their progress is right to the end and object, which is in their way, as it were, and lies just before them; that is, which is feasible and possible, whether it is that which at the first they proposed to themselves or not.

For which reason also such actions are termed *katorqwseiz* to intimate the directness of the way by which they are achieved. Nothing must be thought to belong to a man which does not belong to him, as he is a man. These, the event of purposes, are not things that are required in a man. The nature of man does not profess any such things. The final ends and consummation of actions are nothing at all to a man's nature. The end therefore of a man, or the *summum bonum* whereby that end is fulfilled, cannot consist in the consummation of actions purposed and intended.

Again, concerning these outward worldly things, were it so that any of them properly belonged to man, then it would not belong to man to condemn them and to stand in opposition with them. Neither would he be praiseworthy that can live without them; or he is good, (if these were good indeed) who of his own accord deprives himself of any of them. But we see contrariwise, that the more a man withdraws himself from these where external pomp and greatness consists, or any other like these; or the better he bears with the loss of these, the better he is accounted.

▼

Such as your thoughts and ordinary cogitations are, such will your mind be in time. For the soul receives, as it were, its tincture from the fancies, and imaginations. Dye it therefore and thoroughly soak it with the diligence of these cogitations.

As for example, wherever you may live, it is in your power to live well and happy there. But you may live at the Court, there then also may you live well and happy.

Again, that which everything is made for, he is also made to that, and can only naturally incline to it. That which anything naturally inclines to, there is its end. Where the end of everything consists, his good and benefit consist there also.

Society, therefore, is the proper good of a rational creature. For that, we are made for society. Or can any man make any question of this, that whatever is naturally worse and inferior, is ordinarily subordinated to that which is better? And that those things that are best, are made one for another? And those things that have souls, are better than those that have none? And of those that have, those best that have rational souls?

▼

Desiring the impossible is crazy. But it is impossible that a wicked man should refrain from committing some such things. Neither does anything happen to any man which in the ordinary course of nature as natural to him doesn't happen.

Again, the same things happen to others, also. And truly, if either he that is ignorant that such a thing has happened to him, or he that is ambitious to be commended for his magnanimity, can be patient, and is not grieved: is it not a grievous thing that either ignorance or a vain desire to please and to be commended should be more powerful and effectual than true prudence?

As for the things themselves, they don't touch the soul, neither can they have any access to it. Neither can they of themselves in any way either affect it, or move it. For she herself alone can affect and move herself, and according as the dogma and opinions are, which she does vouchsafe herself; so are those things which, as accessories, have any coexistence with her.

▼

After due consideration, man is nearest to us, as we are

bound to do them good and to bear with them. But as he may oppose any of our true proper actions, so man is to me as only an indifferent thing; even as the sun, or the wind, or some wild beast.

By some of these it may be that some operation or other of mine may be hindered; however, of my mind and resolution itself there can be no let or impediment, by reason of that ordinary constant both exception (or reservation wherewith it inclines) and ready conversion of objects; from that which isn't to that which is, which in the prosecution of its inclinations, as occasion serves, it observes.

For by these the mind turns and converts any impediment whatever to be her aim and purpose. So that what was the impediment before is now the principal object of her working; and that which was in her way before is now her readiest way.

▼

Honor that which is the chiefest and most powerful in the world, and that is it which makes use of all things and governs all things. So also in yourself—honor that which is chiefest, and most powerful, and is of one kind and nature with that which we now speak of. For it is the very same, which being in you, turns all other things to its own use, and by whom your life is also governed.

▼

That which doesn't hurt the city itself can't hurt any citizen. You must remember to apply this rule and make use of every conceit and apprehension of wrong. If the whole city is not hurt by this, neither am I, certainly. And if the whole is not, why should I make it my private grievance?

Consider rather what it is that he is overseen that is thought to have done wrong. Again, often meditate how swiftly all things that subsist, and all things that are done in the world, are carried away, as it were, conveyed out of sight. For both the substances themselves, we see as a flood in a continual flux, and all actions in a perpetual change, the causes themselves, subject to a thousand alterations, neither is there anything almost that may ever be said to be now settled and constant.

Next to this, and which follows upon it, consider both the infinity of the time already past, and the immense vastness of that which is to come, wherein all things are to be resolved and annihilated. Aren't you then very foolish, who for these things are either puffed up with pride, or distracted with cares, or can find in your heart to make such moans as for a thing that would trouble you for a very long time?

Consider the whole universe, where you are but a very little part, and the whole age of the world together, where but a short and very momentary portion is allotted to you, and all the fates and destinies together, of which how much is it that comes to your part and share!

Again: another trespasses against me. Let him look to that. He is master of his own disposition, and of his own operation. I for my part am in the meantime in possession of as much, as the common nature would have me to possess. That which my own nature would have me do, I do.

▼

Don't let that chief commanding part of your soul ever be subject to any variation through anything corporal, either pain or pleasure, and don't let it be mixed with these, but let it both circumscribe itself and confine those affections to their own proper parts and members.

But if at any time they reflect and rebound on the mind and understanding (as it must need in a united and compacted body) then you must not go about resisting sense and feeling, it's natural. However, don't let your understanding to this natural sense and feeling, which whether pleasant or painful to our flesh, is properly nothing to us, except to add an opinion of either good or bad, and all is well.

▼

To live with the gods: He lives with the gods who at all

61

times affords the spectacle of a soul to them, both contented and well pleased with whatever is afforded or allotted to her; and performing whatever is pleasing to that Spirit, whom (being part of himself) Jove has appointed to every man as his overseer and governor.

▼

Don't be angry with someone who has bad breath or body odor. What can he do? His breath is like that naturally, and so are his armpits; and from such, such an effect and such a smell must necessarily proceed.

"Oh, but the man," you say, "has understanding, and might himself know that by standing near he can't help but offend." And you also (God bless you!) have understanding. Let your reasonable faculty work on his reasonable faculty; show him his fault, admonish him. If he hearkens to you, you have cured him, and there will be no more occasion to be angry.

▼

"Where is it that there is neither a loudmouth or a slut?" Why so? As you plan to live, when you have retired to some such place, where there is neither a loudmouth or a slut, so may you here.

And if they will not suffer you, then you may leave your life rather than your calling, but so does one that does not think himself anyways wronged. Only as one would say, Here is smoke; I will get out of it. And what a great matter is this! Now until some such thing forces me out, I will continue free; neither shall any man hinder me to do what I will, and my will shall ever be by the proper nature of a reasonable and sociable creature, regulated and directed.

▼

That rational essence by which the universe is governed is for community and society; and therefore has it both made the things that are worse, for the best, and has allied and knit together those which are best, as it were, in harmony. Don't you see how it has subordinated, and coordinated? And how it has distributed to everything according to its worth? And those which have the preeminence and superiority above all, has it united together into a mutual consent and agreement.

▼

How have you carried yourself towards the gods so far? Towards your parents? Towards your brethren? Towards your wife? Towards your children? Towards your masters? Your foster-fathers? Your friends? Your domestics? Your servants?

Is it so with you, that from now on you have neither by word or deed wronged any of them? Remember through how many things you have already passed, and how many you have been able to endure; so that now the legend of your life is full, and your charge is accomplished.

Again, how many truly good things have you discerned with certainty? How many pleasures, how many pains have you passed over with contempt? How many things eternally glorious have you despised? Towards how many perverse unreasonable men have you carried yourself kindly, and discreetly?

▼

Why should imprudent unlearned souls trouble that which is both learned, and prudent? And which is that that is so? She that understands the beginning and the end, and has the true knowledge of that rational essence that passes through all things subsisting, and through all ages always being the same, disposing and dispensing, as it were, this universe by certain periods of time.

▼

Within a very short time you will be either ashes or a skeleton, and perchance a name; and perchance, not so much as a name. And what is that but an empty sound, and a rebounding echo?

Those things which in this life are dearest to us, and of most account, they are in themselves but vain, putrid, contemptible. The most weighty and serious, if rightly esteemed, but as puppies biting one another. Untoward children, now laughing and then crying.

As for faith, and modesty, and justice, and truth, they long since, as one of the poets has it, have abandoned this spacious earth and retired themselves to heaven. What is it then that keeps you here, if sensible things are so mutable and unsettled? And the senses so obscure, and so fallible? And our souls nothing but an exhalation of blood? And to be in credit among such, is only vanity? What is it that you stay for?

An extinction, or a translation, either of them with a propitious and contented mind. But still when that time comes, what will content you? What else, but to worship and praise the gods, and to do good to men. To bear with them, and to forbear to do them any wrong. And for all external things belonging either to this, your wretched body, or life, to remember that they are neither yours, nor in your power.

▼

You may always go fast, and only if you choose the right way in the course of both your opinions and actions, will you observe a true method. These two things are common to the souls; as it is of God, so it is of men, and of every reasonable creature, first that in their own proper work they cannot be hindered by anything, and secondly, that their happiness consists in a disposition to and in the practice of righteousness; and that in these their desire is terminated.

▼

If this is neither my wicked act or an act that in any way is caused by any wickedness of mine, and that by it the public is not hurt, what does it concern me?

And how can the public be hurt? For you must not be carried altogether by conceit and common opinion. As for help, you must afford that to them after your best ability, and as occasion shall require. Though they sustain damage, but only in these middle or worldly things, don't conceive that they are truly hurt thereby, for that is not right.

But as that old foster-father in the comedy, being now to take his leave does with a great deal of ceremony, require his foster-child's rhombus, or rattle-top, remembering

64

nevertheless that it is but a rhombus; so here also do likewise.

For indeed, what is all this pleading and public bawling for at the courts? Oh, man, have you forgotten what those things are? Yes, but they are things that others much care for, and highly esteem. Will you therefore be a fool, too? Once I was; let that suffice.

▼

Let death surprise me when it will, and where it will. I will be a happy man, nevertheless. For he is a happy man who in his lifetime deals to himself a happy lot and portion. A happy lot and portion is good inclinations of the soul, good desires, and good actions.

▲

Chapter Six
The Disciple

The matter the universe consists of is of itself very tractable and pliable. That rational essence that governs it has in itself no cause to do evil. It has no evil in itself, and can't do anything that is evil. Neither can anything be hurt by it. And all things are done and determined according to its will and prescript.

▼

Make it all the same to you that whether you're half frozen or well warm, whether only napping, or after a full sleep, whether scolded or commended, do your duty. Whether dying or doing something else, for that also, "to die," must among the rest be reckoned as one of the duties and actions of our lives.

▼

Look in, and don't let either the proper quality or the true worth of anything pass you before you fully comprehend it.

▼

All substances soon change, and either they shall be resolved by way of exhalation (if so be that all things shall be reunited into one substance), or as others maintain, they shall be scattered and dispersed.

As for that Rational Essence by which all things are governed, as it best understands itself, both its own disposition, and what it does, and what matter it has to do with and accordingly does everything. So we that don't wonder, if we wonder at many things, the reasons of which we cannot comprehend.

▼

The best kind of revenge is to not to become like them.

▼

Let this be your only joy and your only comfort, from one sociable kind action without intermission to pass to another, God being ever in your mind.

▼

The rational commanding part, as it alone can stir up and turn itself, so it makes both itself to be, and everything that happens, to appear to itself as it wills itself.

▼

According to the nature of the universe, all particular things are not determined according to any other nature, either about compassing and containing; or within, dispersed and contained; or without, depending. Either this universe is a mere confused mass, and an intricate context of things, which shall in time be scattered and dispersed again, or it is a union consisting of order, and administered by Providence.

If the first, why should I desire to continue any longer in this random confusion and co-mixing or blending substances that don't come from the same places? Or why should I care about anything else, since that as soon as it might be, I may be earth again? And why should I trouble myself any more while I seek to please the gods?

Whatever I do, dispersion is my end, and will come upon me whether I will or not. But if the latter is, then I am not religious in vain; then I will be quiet and patient, and put my trust in Him, who is the Governor of all.

▼

Whenever by some hard occurrences you are constrained to be troubled and vexed, return to yourself as soon as you may, and not be out of tune longer than you need to be. That way you will be better able to keep your part another time, and to maintain the harmony, if you use yourself to this continually; once out, presently to have recourse to it, and to begin again.

▼

If you had both a stepmother and a living natural mother, you would honor and respect her also; nevertheless to your own natural mother would you seek refuge, and her recourse would be continual.

So let the court and your philosophy be to you. Have recourse to it often, and comfort yourself in her, by whom it is that those other things are made tolerable to you, and you also in those things not intolerable to others.

▼

How marvelously useful it is for a man to give himself meats, and all such things that are for the mouth, under a right apprehension and imagination! For example: This is the carcass of a fish; this of a bird; and this of a hog. And again more generally; this syrup, this excellent highly commended wine, is but the bare juice of an ordinary grape. This purple robe, but sheep's hairs, dyed with the blood of a shellfish.

So for coitus, it is but the attrition of an ordinary base entrails, and the excretion of a little vile snot, with a certain kind of convulsion, according to Hippocrates; his opinion. How excellent useful are these lively fancies and representations of things, thus penetrating and passing through the objects, to make their true nature known and apparent!

You must use this all your life long, and upon all occasions: and then specially, when matters are apprehended as of great worth and respect, your care must be to uncover them, and to behold their vileness, and to take away from them all those serious circumstances and expressions under which they made so grave a show. For outward pomp and appearance is a great juggler; and then especially are you in danger of being beguiled by it the most, when (to a man's thinking) you seem to be most employed about matters of moment.

▼

See what Crates says concerning Xenocrates himself.[11]

▼

Those things which the common sort of people admire are, most of them, such things as are very general, and may be comprehended under things merely natural or naturally affected and qualified, as stones, wood, figs, vines, olives.

Those that are admired by the more moderate and restrained, are comprehended under things animated, as flocks and herds. Those that are yet more gentle and curious, their admiration is commonly confined to reasonable creatures only. Not in general as they are reasonable, but as they are capable of are, or of some craft and subtle invention. Perchance to barely be reasonable creatures, as they that delight in the possession of many slaves.

But he that honors a reasonable soul in general, as it is reasonable and naturally sociable, little regards anything else, and above all things is careful to preserve his own, in the continual habit and exercise both of reason and sociableness. Thereby cooperates with him of whose nature he also participates; God.

▼

Some things are in a hurry to exist, and others to exist no more. And even whatever now is, some part of it has already perished. Perpetual fluxes and alterations renew the world, as the perpetual course of time makes the age of the world (of itself infinite[12]) to appear always fresh and new.

In such a flux and course of all things, what of these things that any man should regard goes away so fast, since among all there is not any that a man may fasten and fix upon?

As if a man would settle his affection upon some ordinary sparrow living by him, who is no sooner seen, than out of sight. For we must not think otherwise of our lives, than as a mere exhalation of blood, or of an ordinary respiration of air.

For what in our common apprehension is, to breathe in

69

the air and to breathe it out again, which we do daily. So much it is and no more, at once to breathe out all your respiratory faculties into that common air from where but lately (as being but from yesterday, and today), you first breathed it in, and with it, life.

▼

It is surely not vegetative spiration, which plants have, that in this life should be so dear to us; nor sensitive respiration, the proper life of beasts, both tame and wild; nor this our imaginative faculty; nor that we are subject to be led and carried up and down by the strength of our sensual appetites; or that we can gather, and live together; or that we can feed: for that in effect is no better than that we can defecate.

What is it, then, that should be dear to us? To hear a clattering noise? If not that, then neither is it to be applauded by the tongues of men. For the praises of many tongues, is in effect no better than the clattering of so many tongues. If it's not applause, what is there remaining that should be dear to you?

This is what I think: that in all your motions and actions you are moved, and restrained according to your own true natural constitution and construction only. And to this even ordinary arts and professions lead us. For it is that which every art aims at, that whatever it is, that is by effected and prepared, may be fit for that work that it is prepared for.

This is the end that he that dresses the vine, and he that takes upon himself either to tame colts, or to train dogs, aims at. What else does the education of children, and all learned professions tend to? Certainly then it is that, which should be dear to us also.

If in this particular it goes well with you, don't care about obtaining other things. But isn't it so, that you can't help but respect other things, too? Then can you truly be free? Then you can't have self-content. Then you will ever be subject to passions.

For it is not possible, but that you must be envious, and jealous, and suspicious of them whom you know can bereave you of such things; and again, a secret underminer of them, whom you see in present possession of that which is dear to you.

In short, he must of necessity be full of confusion within himself, and often accuse the gods, whosoever stands in need of these things. But if you will honor and respect your mind only, that will make you acceptable towards yourself, towards your friends very tractable; and conformable and concordant with the gods; that is, accepting with praises whatever they shall think good to appoint and give to you.

▼

Under, above, and about, are the motions of the elements; but the motion of virtue is none of those motions, but is somewhat more excellent and divine. Whose way (to speed and prosper in it) must be through a way that is not easily comprehended.

▼

Who can choose but wonder at them? They will not speak well of them that are at the same time with them, and live with them; yet they themselves are very ambitious, that they that shall follow whom they have never seen, nor shall ever see, should speak well of them. As if a man should grieve that he has not been commended by them who lived before him.

▼

Never conceive anything impossible to a man that you can't do, or not without much difficulty do; but whatever in general you can conceive possible and proper to any man, think that very possible to you as well.

▼

Suppose that at the wrestling school somebody has torn you with his nails and broken your head. Well, you are wounded. Yet you don't exclaim; you are not offended with him. You do not suspect him for it afterwards, as one who looks to do you mischief.

Yet even then, though you did your best to save yourself from him, but not from him as an enemy. It is not by way of any suspicious indignation, but by way of gentle and friendly declination. Keep the same mind and disposition in other parts of your life also.

For there are many things that we must conceive of and comprehend, as though we had had to do with an antagonist at the wrestling school. For as I said, it is very possible for us to avoid and decline, though we neither suspect, nor hate.

▼

If anyone should reprove me, and make it apparent to me that in any either opinion or action of mine I err, I will most gladly retract it. For it is the truth that I seek after, by which I am sure that no man was hurt; and just as sure, that he who is hurt is one that continues in any error or ignorance whatever.

▼

I, for my part, will do what belongs to me. As for other things, whether things insensible or things irrational, or if rational, yet deceived and ignorant of the true way, they shall not trouble or distract me.

For as for those creatures which are not endued with reason and all other things, and matters of the world whatever, I freely and generously make use of them.

And as for men, towards them as naturally partakers of the same reason, my care is to carry myself sociably. But whatever it is that you are about, remember to call on the gods. And as for the time how long you will live to do these things, let it be altogether indifferent to you, for even three such hours are sufficient.

▼

Alexander of Macedon, and he that dressed his mules, when once dead both came to one. For either they were both resumed into those original rational essences from whence all things in the world are propagated; or both after one fashion were scattered into atoms.

▼

Consider how many different things, whether they concern our bodies or our souls, in a moment of time come to pass in every one of us. You will not wonder if many more things or rather all things that are done can at one time subsist, and coexist in that both one and general, which we call the world.

▼

If anyone should ask you how the word "Antoninus" is written, would you not quickly fix your attention to it, and utter out in order every letter of it? And if any shall begin to gainsay you and quarrel with you about it, will you quarrel with him again, or rather go on meekly as you had begun, until you have numbered out every letter?

Then likewise remember that every duty that belongs to a man consists of some certain letters or numbers, as it were, to which keeping yourself without any noise or tumult you must proceed in an orderly manner to your proposed end, forbearing to quarrel with him that would quarrel and fall out with you.

▼

Isn't it a cruel thing to forbid men to do those things which they conceive to agree best with their own natures, and to tend most to their own proper good as it behooves them? But you, after a sort, deny them this liberty as often as you are angry with them for their misbehavior.

For surely they are led to those sins, whatever they are, as to their proper good and commodity. But it is not so, although you may object. You should therefore teach them better, and make it appear to them, but not be angry with them.

▼

Death is a cessation from the impression of the senses, the tyranny of the passions, the errors of the mind, and the servitude of the body.

If in this kind of life your body is able to hold out, it would be a shame if your soul should faint first, and give over. Take heed, lest in time you become a mere Caesar of a philosopher, and receive a new tincture from the court. For it may happen if you don't take heed.

Therefore, keep yourself truly simple, good, sincere, grave, free from all ostentation, a lover of that which is just, religious, kind, tender hearted, strong and vigorous, to undergo anything that becomes you. Endeavor to continue such, as philosophy (had you wholly and constantly applied yourself to it) would have made, and secured you.

Worship the gods, procure the welfare of men; this life is short. Charitable actions, and a holy disposition, is the only fruit of this earthly life.

▼

Do all things as become the disciple of Antoninus Pius[13]. Remember his resolute constancy in things that he did according to reason, his equability in all things, his sanctity. The cheerfulness of his countenance, his sweetness, and how free he was from all vanity. How careful to come to the true and exact knowledge of matters in hand, and how he would by no means give over till he fully understood, and plainly understand the whole state of the business; and how patiently, and without any argument he would bear with those who unjustly condemn him. How he would never be over heavy in anything, nor give ear to slanders and false accusations, but examine and observe with best diligence the several actions and dispositions of men.

Again, how he was no backbiter, nor easily frightened, nor suspicious. In his language he was free from all affectation and curiosity, and how easily he would content himself with few things, as lodging, bedding, clothing, and ordinary nourishment, and attendance.

How able he was to endure labor, how patient. Able through his spare diet to continue from morning to evening without any necessity of withdrawing before his accustomed hours to the necessities of nature.

His uniformity and constancy in matter of friendship. How he would bear with them that with all boldness and liberty opposed his opinions, and even rejoiced if any man could better advise him. Lastly, how religious he was without superstition.

All these things of him remember, that whenever your last hour shall come upon you, it may find you, as it did him, ready for it in the possession of a good conscience.

▼

Stir up your mind, and recall your wits again from your natural dreams and visions, and when you are perfectly awakened, and can see that they were only dreams that troubled you; as one newly awakened out of another kind of sleep, look at these worldly things with the same mind as you did at those that you saw in your sleep.

▼

I consist of body and soul. To my body all things are indifferent, for of itself it can't affect one thing more than another with apprehension of any difference; as for my mind, all things which are not within the verge of her own operation, are indifferent to her, and for her own operations, those altogether depend of her. Neither does she busy herself about any but those that are present, for as for future and past operations, those also are now at this present indifferent to her.

▼

As long as the foot does that which belongs to it to do, and the hand that which belongs to it, their labor, whatever it is, isn't unnatural. So as long as a man does that which is

75

proper for a man, his labor cannot be against nature; and if it isn't against nature, then neither is it harmful to him.

But if it were so that happiness consisted in pleasure, how is it that notorious robbers, impure abominable livers, parricides, and tyrants, in so large a measure have pleasures?

▼

Don't you see how even those that profess the arts of a mechanic are in some respect no better than mere idiots, yet they stick close to the course of their trade, neither can they find in their heart to decline from it? And isn't it a grievous thing that an architect, or a physician shall respect the course and mysteries of their profession, more than a man the proper course and condition of his own nature, reason, which is common to him and to the gods?

▼

Asia, Europe—what are they but corners of the whole world, of which the whole sea is but as one drop, and the great Mount Athos but as a clod, as all present time is but as one point of eternity?

All are petty things; all things that are soon altered, soon perished. And all things come from one beginning; either all severally and particularly deliberated and resolved upon by the general ruler and governor of all, or all by necessary consequence. So that the dreadful hiatus of a gaping lion, and all poison, and all harmful things, are only (as the thorn and the mire) the necessary consequences of goodly fair things.

Therefore don't think of these as things as contrary to those which you greatly honor and respect, but consider in your mind the true fountain of everything.

▼

He that sees the things that exist now has seen all that either ever was or ever will be, for all things are of one kind; and all are like one another. Meditate often on the connection of all things in the world, and on the mutual relation that they have to one another. For all things are after a sort folded and involved, one within another, and by these means all agree well together. For one thing is consequent to another, by local motion, by natural hidden combination and agreement, and by substantial union, or reduction of all substances into one.

▼

Fit and accommodate yourself to that state and to those occurrences which destiny has annexed to you, and love those men whom your fate it is to live with, but love them truly. An instrument, a tool, a utensil, whatever it is, if it's fit for the purpose it was made for, it is as it should be, though whoever made and fitted it is out of sight and gone.

But in natural things, that power which has framed and fitted them, abides within them still; for which reason she ought also the more to be respected, and we are the more obliged (if we may live and pass our time according to her purpose and intention) to think that all is well with us, and according to our own minds. After this manner also, and in this respect it is, that he that is all in all enjoys his happiness.

▼

Whatever things are not within your proper power and jurisdiction will either encompass or avoid you, if you will propose to yourself any of those things as either good, or evil. It must be that according as you will, either fall into that which you think evil, or miss that which you think good, so will you be ready both to complain of the gods, and to hate those men, who either shall be so indeed, or shall by your be suspected as the cause either of your missing of the one, or falling into the other.

And indeed we must commit many evils if we incline to any of these things, more or less, with an opinion of any difference. But if we mind and fancy only those things as good and bad which wholly depend of our own wills, there is no more occasion why we should either murmur against the gods, or be at enmity with any man.

We all work to one effect, some willingly, and with a rational apprehension of what we do, others without any such knowledge. As I think Heraclitus, in one place, speaks of them that sleep, that even they do work in their kind, and confer to the general operations of the world.

HERACLITVS.

One man therefore co-operates after one sort, and another after another sort; but even he that murmurs, and resists and hinders; even he as much as any cooperates. For the world also stood in need of such.

Now consider which among these you will rank yourself. For as for him who is the Administrator of all, he will make good use of you whether you want to or not, and make you (as a part and member of the whole) cooperate with him, that whatever you do shall turn to the furtherance of his own counsels and resolutions.

But don't be ashamed of such a part of the whole, as that vile and ridiculous verse (which Chrysippus in one place mentions) is a part of the comedy.

▼

Does either the sun take it upon himself to do that which belongs to the rain? Or his son Aesculapius that to which the earth properly belongs? How is it with every one of the stars in particular? Though they all differ one from another, and have their several charges and functions by themselves, do they not all nevertheless concur and cooperate to one end?

▼

If the gods have deliberated in particular of those things that should happen to me, I must stand to their deliberation as discrete and wise. For that a God should be an imprudent God is a thing that's hard to imagine—why should they resolve to do me harm? For what profit either to them or the universe (which they specially take care for) could arise from it?

But if it is that they have not deliberated of me in particular, certainly they have of the whole in general, and those things which in consequence and coherence of this general deliberation happen to me in particular, I am bound to embrace and accept.

But if it is that they have not deliberated at all (which indeed is very irreligious for any man to believe, for then let us neither sacrifice, nor pray, nor respect our oaths, neither let us any more use any of those things which we persuaded of the presence and secret conversation of the gods among us, daily use and practice) but, I say, if it is that they have not indeed either in general, or particular deliberated of any of those things that happen to us in this world. Yet God be thanked for those things that concern myself, it is lawful for me to deliberate myself, and all my deliberation is but concerning that which may be to me most profitable.

Now that is most profitable to every one which is according to his own constitution and nature. And my nature is to be rational in all my actions and as a good and natural member of a city and commonwealth towards my fellow members ever to be sociably and kindly disposed and affected. As I am Antoninus, my city and country is Rome; as a man, the whole world. Those things therefore that are expedient and profitable to those cities, are the only things that are good and expedient for me.

▼

Whatever in any kind happens to anyone is expedient to the whole. And therefore, much to make us content might suffice, that it is expedient for the whole in general. But yet this also will you generally perceive, if you diligently take heed, that whatever happens to any one man or men... And now I am content that the word expedient, should more generally be understood of those things which we otherwise call middle things, or things indifferent; as health, wealth, and the like.

▼

When you're presented with the ordinary shows of the theater and of other such places, they affect you as the same things still seen, and in the same fashion, make the sight ungrateful and tedious; so must all the things that we see all our life long affect us. For all things, above and below, are still the same, and from the same causes. When, then, will there be an end?

▼

Let the several deaths of all sorts men, and of all sorts of professions, and of all sort of nations, be a perpetual object of your thoughts, so that you may even come down to Philistio, Phoebus, and Origanion. Pass now to other generations. There, after many changes of all sorts, where so many brave orators are; where so many grave philosophers; Heraclitus, Pythagoras, Socrates. Where so many heroes of the old times; and then so many brave captains of the latter times; and so many kings.

After all these, where Eudoxus, Hipparchus, Archimedes; where so many other sharp, generous, industrious, subtle, peremptory dispositions; and among others, even they, that have been the greatest scoffers and deriders of the frailty and brevity of this our human life; as Menippus, and others, as many as there have been such as he.

Of all these, consider that they are all long since dead and gone. And what do they suffer by it? No, they that have not so much as a name remaining, what are they the worse for it? One thing there is, and that only, which is worth our while in this world, and ought by us much to be esteemed; and that is, according to truth and righteousness, meekly and lovingly to converse with false, and unrighteous men.

▼

When you want to comfort and cheer yourself, call to mind the several gifts and virtues of those who you converse with daily. For example, the industry of the one, the modesty of another, the liberality of a third, of another some other thing. For nothing can so much rejoice you as the resemblances and parallels of several virtues, visible and eminent in the dispositions of those who live with you. Especially when all at once, as near as may be, they represent themselves to you. And therefore you must have them always in a readiness.

▼

Do you grieve that you only weigh but so many pounds, and rather not three hundred? Just as much reason have you to grieve that you must live but so many years, and not longer. For as for bulk and substance you content yourself with that proportion of it that is allotted to you, so you should for time.

▼

Let us endeavor most to persuade them, but if reason and justice lead you to it, do it, though they're never so much against it. But if any shall by force withstand you, and hinder you in it, convert your virtuous inclination from one object to another, from justice to contented equanimity, and cheerful patience: so that what in the one is your hindrance, you may make use of it for the exercise of another virtue and remember that it was with due exception, and reservation, that you inclined and desired at first.

For you didn't set your mind on impossible things. Upon what then? That all your desires might ever be moderated with this due kind of reservation. And this you have, and may always obtain, whether the thing is desired be in your power or not. And what do I care for more, if that for which I was born and brought forth into the world (to rule all my desires with reason and discretion) may be?

▼

The ambitious suppose that another man's act, praise

and applause, to be his own happiness; the voluptuous his own sense and feeling; but he that is wise, his own action.

▼

It is absolutely in your power to exclude all manner of conceit and opinion, as concerning this matter; and by the same means, to exclude all grief and sorrow from your soul. For as for the things and objects themselves, they of themselves have no such power, whereby to beget and force upon us any opinion at all.

▼

Use yourself when any man speaks to you so as to hearken to him, so that in the interim you don't give way to any other thoughts; that so you may as far as is possible seem fixed and fastened to his very soul, whoever he is that speaks to you.

▼

That which is not good for the beehive can't be good for the bee.

▼

Will either passengers or patients find fault and complain, either one if he is well transported, or the others if well cured? Do they take care for any more than this; the one, that their shipmaster may bring them safe to land, and the other, that their physician may cause their recovery?

▼

How many of them who came into the world at the same time as I did are already gone out of it?

▼

To them that are sick of the jaundice, honey seems bitter; and to them that are bitten by a mad dog, the water terrible; and to children, a little ball seems a fine thing. And why then should I be angry? Or do I think that error and false opinion is less powerful to make men transgress, than either cholera, being immoderate and excessive, to cause the jaundice; or poison, to cause rage?

▼

No man can hinder you from living as your nature requires. Nothing can happen to you but what the common good of nature requires.

▼

What manner of men they are who seek to please, and what to get, and by what actions: how soon time will cover and bury all things, and how many it has already buried!

▲

Chapter Seven
Spend Every Day As If It Were Your Last

What is wickedness? It is that which often many times you have already seen and known in the world. And so often as anything happens that might otherwise trouble you, let this memento presently come to your mind, that it is that which you have already often seen and known.

Generally, above and below, you will find but the same things. The very same things that ancient stories, middle age stories, and fresh stories are full of. Towns are full, and houses full. There is nothing that is new. All things that are, are both usual and of little continuance.

▼

What fear is there that your dogma or philosophical resolutions and conclusions should become dead in you and lose their proper power and efficacy to make your life happy, as long as those proper and correlative fancies, and representations of things on which they mutually depend (which continually to stir up and revive is in your power) are still kept fresh and alive? It is in my power concerning this thing that is happened, whatever it is, to conceive that which is right and true. If it is, then why am I troubled? Those things that are without my understanding, are nothing to it at all, and that is it only which properly concerns me. Always keep this in mind and you will always be right.

▼

That which most men would think themselves most happy with and would prefer before all things, if the gods would grant it to them after their deaths, you may while you live grant to yourself; to live again. See the things of the world again, as you have already seen them. For what else is it to live again?

Public shows and solemnities with much pomp and vanity, stage plays, flocks and herds; conflicts and contentions. A bone thrown to a company of hungry curs. A bait for greedy fishes. The painfulness, and continual burden-bearing of wretched ants, the running to and fro of terrified mice.

Little puppets drawn up and down with wires and nerves: these are the objects of the world, and among all these you must stand steadfast, meekly affected, and free from all manner of indignation, with this right correct thinking and apprehension. That is the worth is of those things which a man affects, so is in very deed every man's worth, more or less.

▼

The things that are spoken must be conceived and understood word after word, every one by itself, and so the things that are done, purpose after purpose, every one by itself likewise. And as in matter of purposes and actions, we must presently see what the proper use and relation of every one is, so of words must we be as ready, to consider of every one what is the true meaning, and signification of it according to truth and nature, however it's taken in common use.

▼

Is my reason and understanding sufficient for this, or not? If it is sufficient, without any private applause or public ostentation as of an instrument which by nature I am provided, I will make use of it for the work in hand, as of an instrument which by nature I am provided. if it is not, and that otherwise it doesn't belong to me particularly as a private duty, I will either give it over, and leave it to some other that can do it better, or I will endeavor at it, but with the help of some other, who with the joint help of my reason is able to bring something to pass that will now be seasonable and useful for the common good.

For whatever I do either by myself or with some other, the only thing that I must intend is that it be good and expedient for the public. For as for praise, consider how many who once were much commended, are now already quite forgotten, yes, they that commended them, how even they themselves are long since dead and gone. Don't be ashamed, therefore, whenever you must use the help of others. For whatever it is that lies upon you to change, you must propose it to yourself, as the scaling of walls is to a soldier.

And what if you, through either lameness or some other impediment, are not able to reach to the top of the battlements alone, which with the help of another you may. Will you therefore give it over, or go about it with less courage and alacrity, because you can't do it all alone?

▼

Don't let future things trouble you, for if necessity requires that they come to pass, you will (whenever that is) be provided for them with the same reason by which whatever is now present is made both tolerable and acceptable to you. All things are linked and knitted together, and the knot is sacred, neither is there anything in the world that is not kind and natural in regard of any other thing, or, that has not some kind of reference and natural correspondence with whatever is in the world besides.

For all things are ranked together, and by that decency of its due place and order that each particular observes, they all concur together to the making of one and the same cosmos or world. As if you said, a comely piece, or an orderly composition.

For all things throughout, there is but one order; and through all things, one and the same God, the same substance and the same law. There is one common reason, and one common truth, that belongs to all reasonable creatures, for neither is there save one perfection of all creatures that are of the same kind, and partakers of the same reason.

▼

Material things soon vanish away into the common substance of the whole; and whatever is formal, or whatever animates that which is material, is soon resumed into the common reason of the whole; and the fame and memory of anything is soon swallowed up by the general age and duration of the whole.

▼

To a reasonable creature, the same action is both according to nature, and according to reason.

▼

Straight of itself, not made straight.

▼

As several members are united in one body, so are reasonable creatures in a body that is divided and dispersed all made and prepared for one common operation. And this you will apprehend the better if you will use yourself often to say to yourself, I am *meloz*, or a member of the mass and body of reasonable substances.

But if you will say I am *meroz*, or a part, you do not yet love men from your heart. The joy that you take in the exercise of bounty is not yet grounded upon a due rationalization and right apprehension of the nature of things. You exercise it as yet barely upon this ground, as a thing convenient and fitting; not as doing good to yourself when you do good to others.

▼

Of external things, accidents happen to that which can suffer by external things. Those things that suffer let them complain themselves, if they will. As for me, as long as I don't conceive such a thing, that that which is happened is evil, I have suffered no harm; and it is in my power not to conceive any such thing.

▼

Whatever any man either does or says, you must be good; not for any man's sake, but for your own nature's sake, as if either gold or the emerald or purple should ever be saying to themselves, "whatever any man either does or says, I must still be an emerald, and I must keep my color."

▼

This will always be my comfort and security: my understanding that rules over all will not of itself bring trouble and vexation upon itself. This I say, it will not put itself in any fear, it will not lead itself into any lust.

87

If it is in the power of any other to compel it to fear, or to grieve, it is free for him to use his power. But if it's sure of itself, through some false opinion or supposition incline itself to any such disposition, there is no fear.

For as for the body, why should I make the grief of my body to be the grief of my mind? If that itself can either fear or complain, let it. But as for the soul, which indeed, can only be truly sensible of either fear or grief; to which only it belongs according to its different imaginations and opinions, to admit of either of these or of their contraries; you may look to that yourself, that it suffers nothing.

Induce her not to any such opinion or persuasion. The understanding is of itself sufficient itself, and needs not (if itself does not bring itself to need) any other thing besides itself, and by consequence as it needs nothing, so neither can it be troubled or hindered by anything, if itself does not trouble and hinder itself.

▼

Whatever will fall, falls on what will feel the effects; whoever feels the effects may complain. Unless I think what has happened is evil, and I am not hurt by it, it is in my power to not think it was evil.

▼

Is any man so foolish as to fear change, to which all things that once didn't exist owe their being? And what is it that is more pleasing and more familiar to the nature of the universe?

How could you use your ordinary hot baths, should not the wood that heated them first be changed? How could you receive any nourishment from those things that you have eaten if they should not be changed? Can anything else that is useful and profitable be created without change?

Then how don't you perceive that for you also, by death comes to change, is a thing of the very same nature, and as is necessary for the nature of the universe?

Through the substance of the universe, as through a torrent passes all particular bodies, all being of the same nature, and all joint workers with the universe itself, as in one of our bodies are so many members among themselves. How many such as Chrysippus, how many such as Socrates, how many such as Epictetus, has the age of the world long since swallowed up and devoured?

Let this, be it either men or businesses, that you have occasion to think of, to the end that your thoughts be not distracted and your mind too earnestly set upon anything, upon every such occasion presently come to your mind. Only one thing will be the object of all my thoughts and cares, that I myself do nothing which to the proper constitution of man (either in regard of the thing itself, or in regard of the manner, or of the time of doing), is contrary.

The time when you will have forgotten all things is at hand. And that time is also at hand when you yourself will be forgotten by all. While you are, apply yourself to that especially which to man as he is a man, is most proper and agreeable, and that is for a man even to love them that transgress against him.

This shall be, if at the same time that any such thing happens, you should call to mind that they are your kinsmen; that it is through ignorance and against their wills that they sin; and that within a very short while after, both you and he shall be no more. But above all things, that he has not done you any hurt; for that by him your mind and understanding is not made worse or more vile than it was before.

▼

The nature of the universe, of the common substance of all things is as it were of so much wax, and has now perchance formed a horse. Then, destroying that figure, has now tempered and fashioned the matter of it into the form and substance of a tree. Then that again into the form and substance of a man, and then that again into some other. Now every one of these does exist but for a very little while.

As for dissolution, if it is no grievous thing to the chest or trunk to be joined together, why should it be more grievous to be put asunder?

▼

An angry countenance is much against nature, and it is often the proper countenance of them that are at the point of death. But were it so that all anger and passion were so thoroughly quenched in you, that it were altogether impossible to kindle it any more, you must not rest satisfied, but further endeavor by good consequence of true reasoning, perfectly to conceive and understand that all anger and passion is against reason.

For if you will not be sensible of your innocence; if that also will be gone from you, the comfort of a good conscience that you do everything according to reason. What should you live any longer for?

All things that now you see are but for a moment. That nature, by which all things in the world are administered, will soon bring change and alteration upon them, and then of their substances make other things like them. Then soon after, others again of the matter and substance of these, that so by these means the world may still appear fresh and new.

▼

Whenever any man trespasses against another, presently consider with yourself what it was that he thought to be good, which was actually, when he trespassed. For when you know this, you will pity him and have no occasion either to wonder, or to be angry.

For either you yourself still live in that error and ignorance, as that you supposed either that very thing that he does, or some other like worldly thing, to be good; and so you are bound to pardon him if he has done that which you would have done yourself.

Or if it is that you don't suppose the same things to be good or evil that he does, how can you but be gentle to him, who is in error?

▼

Don't imagine future things as though they were present, but only those that actually are present. Take some aside, so that you take the most benefit from it, and consider of them particularly how badly you would want them if they were not present.

But take heed withal, lest that while you settle your contentment in present things, that in time you grow to prize them too much, as that the want of them (whenever it should fall out) should be a trouble and a vexation to you. Wind up yourself into yourself.

Such is the nature of your reasonable commanding part, as that if it exercises justice, and has by that means tranquility within itself, it rests fully satisfied with itself without any other thing.

▼

Wipe off all opinion. Stop the force and violence of unreasonable lusts and affections. Circumscribe the present time, examine whatever it is that happened, either to yourself or to another: divide all present objects, either in that which is formal or material; think of the last hour.

That which your neighbor has committed, where the guilt of it lies, there let it rest. Examine in order whatever is spoken. Let your mind penetrate both into the effects and into the causes.

Rejoice yourself with true simplicity and modesty; and that all middle things between virtue and vice are indifferent to you. Finally, love mankind; obey God.

▼

"All things," he says, "are by certain order and appointment, and of the elements only."

It will suffice to remember that all things in general are by a certain order and appointment, if only but a few. And as concerning death, that either dispersion, or the atoms, or annihilation, or extinction, or translation will ensue.

91

And as concerning pain, that that which is intolerable is soon ended by death, and that which lasts a long time must be tolerable. And that the mind, in the meantime (which is all in all) may by way of inclusion, or interception, by stopping all manner of commerce and sympathy with the body, still retain its own tranquility.

Your understanding is not made worse by it. As for those parts that suffer, let them, if they can, declare their grief themselves.

As for praise and commendation, view their mind and understanding, what state they are in; what kind of things they flee from, and what things they seek after: and that as in the seaside, whatever was before to be seen, is by the continual succession of new heaps of sand cast up one upon another, soon hid and covered; so in this life, all former things by those which immediately succeed.

▼

From Plato: "He then whose mind is endowed with true magnanimity, who has accustomed himself to the contemplation both of all times, and of all things in general; can this mortal life (you think) seem any great matter to him? It is not possible, he answered. Then neither will such a one account death a grievous thing? By no means."

▼

From Antisthenes: "It is a princely thing to do well, and to be ill-spoken of. It is a shameful thing that mind should concern itself with the beauty of the face, not bestow so much care upon itself, as to fashion itself, and to dress itself as best becomes it."

▼

From several poets and comics: "It will avail you but

92

little to turn your anger and indignation upon the things that have befallen you. For as for them, they are not sensible of it. You will only make yourself a laughingstock; both to the gods and to men.

"Our life is reaped like a ripe ear of corn; one is yet standing and another is down. But if it is that I and my children be neglected by the gods, there is some reason even for that. As long as right and equity is of my side, not to lament with them, not to tremble."

▼

From Plato: "My answer, full of justice and equity, should be this: your speech is not right, Oh man, if you suppose that he that is of any worth at all should apprehend either life or death as a matter of great hazard and danger; and should not make this rather his only care, to examine his own actions, whether just or unjust: whether actions are of a good, or of a wicked man!

"For this case in very truth stands, oh you men of Athens. What place or station a man either has chosen to himself, judging it best for himself; or is by lawful authority put and settled in, therein do I think (all appearance of danger notwithstanding) that he should continue, as one who fears neither death, nor anything else, so much as he fears to commit anything that is vicious and shameful.

"But, Oh noble sir, I pray you consider whether true generosity and true happiness do not consist in something else, rather than in the preservation either of our, or other men's lives. For it is not the part of a man that is a man indeed to desire to live long or to make much of his life while he lives, but rather (he that is such) will in these things wholly refer himself to the gods, and believing that which every woman can tell him, that no man can escape death; the only thing that he takes thought and care for is this, that what time he lives, he may live as well and as virtuously as he can possibly.

"To look about, and with the eyes following the course of the stars and planets as though you would run with them;

and to perpetually pay attention to the several changes of the elements, one into another. For such fancies and imaginations help much to purge away the dross and filth of this, our earthly life."

That also is a fine passage of Plato's, where he speaks of worldly things in these words: "you must also, as from some higher place, look down, as it were, upon the things of this world, as flocks, armies, husbandmen's labors, marriages, divorces, generations, deaths, the tumults of courts and places of adjudications; desert places; the several nations of barbarians, public festivals, mournings, fairs, markets." How all things upon earth are pell mell, and how miraculously things contrary to one to another concur to the beauty and perfection of this universe.

▼

Look back on things of former ages, as upon the manifold changes and conversions of several monarchies and commonwealths. We may also foresee future things, for they will all be of the same kind; neither is it possible that they should leave the tune or break the concert that is now begun, as it were, by these things that are now done and brought to pass in the world.

It comes all to one therefore, whether a man be a spectator of the things of this life but forty years, or whether he sees them ten thousand years together. For what shall he see more? "And as for those parts that came from the earth, they shall return to the earth again; and those that came from heaven, they also shall return to those heavenly places."

Whether it be a mere dissolution and unbinding of the manifold intricacies and entanglements of the confused atoms; or some such dispersion of the simple and incorruptible elements... "With meats and drinks and diverse charms, they seek to divert the channel, that they might not die. Yet we must need to endure that blast of wind that comes from above, though we toil and labor never so much."

▼

He has a stronger body and is a better wrestler than I. So what? Is he more bountiful? Is he more modest? Does he bear all adverse chances with more equanimity, or with his neighbor's offenses with more meekness and gentleness than I?

▼

Where a matter may be agreeably finished by reason, to which both the gods and men is common, there can be no just cause of grief or sorrow. For where the fruit and benefit of an action began and prosecuted according to the proper constitution of man may be reaped and obtained, or is sure and certain, it is against reason that any damage should there be suspected.

In all places, and at all times, it is in your power to religiously embrace whatever by God's appointment has happened to you, and justly to converse with those men whom you have to deal with, and accurately to examine every fancy that presents itself, that nothing may slip and steal in before you have rightly comprehended the true nature of it.

▼

Don't look to other men's minds and understandings, but look forward where nature, both of the universe and in those things that happen to you, and you in particular in those things that you do: it leads and direct you. Now, every one is bound to do that which is consequent and agreeable to the end which by his true natural constitution he was ordained to.

As for all other things, they are ordained for the use of reasonable creatures. As in all things we see that that which is worse and inferior, is made for that which is better. Reasonable creatures are ordained one for another. That therefore which is chief in every man's constitution is that he intend the common good.

The second is, that he doesn't yield to any lusts and motions of the flesh. For it is the part and privilege of the reasonable and intellectual faculty, that she can so bound herself, so that neither the sensitive, nor the appetitive faculties may not anyways prevail upon her. For both these are brutish.

And therefore over both she challenges mastery, and if in her right temper cannot endure to be subject to either, anyway. And this is indeed most just. For by nature she was ordained to command all in the body.

The third thing proper to man by his constitution is to avoid all rashness, and not to be subject to error. Then let the mind apply herself and go straight on to these things, then, without any distraction about other things, and she has her end, and by consequent her happiness.

▼

As one who had lived and were now to die, bestow whatever is yet remaining fully as a gracious surplus on top of a virtuous life. Love and affect that only, whatever it is that happens and is appointed to you by the fates. For what can be more reasonable?

And as anything happens to you by way of cross, or calamity, presently call to mind and set before your eyes the examples of some other men to whom the same thing likewise once happened. Well, what did they do? They grieved; they wondered; they complained. And where are they now? All dead and gone. Will you also be like one of them?

Or rather leaving to men of the world (whose life both in regard of themselves, and them that they converse with, is nothing but mere mutability; or men of as fickle minds, as fickle bodies; ever changing and soon changed themselves) let it be your only care and study how to make a correct use of all such accidents. For there is good use to be made of them, and they will prove fit matter for you to work on, if it's both your care and your desire, that whatever you do, you yourself may like and approve yourself for it.

And both these, see that you remember well, according as the diversity of the matter of the action that you are about shall require. Look within; within is the fountain of all good.

Such a fountain, where springing waters can never fail, so you dig still deeper and deeper.

▼

You must also use yourself to keep your body fixed and steady; free from all loose, unstable motion or posture. And as on your face and looks, your mind easily has power over them to keep them to that which is grave and decent; so let it challenge the same power over the whole body as well. But also observe all things like that, as that it is without any manner of affectation.

▼

The art of true living in this world is more like a wrestler's than a dancer's practice. For in this they both agree, to teach a man whatever falls upon him that he may be ready for it, and that nothing may cast him down.

▼

You must continually ponder and consider with yourself what manner of men they are, and what is their present state of their minds and understandings, whose good word and testimony you desire. For then neither will you see cause to complain of them that offend against their will, or find any want of their applause, if once you just penetrate into the true force and ground, both of their opinions and of their desires.

"No soul," says he, "is willingly bereft of the truth," and by consequent, neither of justice, or temperance, or kindness, and mildness; nor of anything that is of the same kind. It is most needful that you should always remember this. For if so, you will be far more gentle and moderate towards all men.

▼

Whatever pain you're in, let this presently come to your mind, that it isn't anything you need to be ashamed of, and neither is it a thing where your understanding, that has the government of all, can be made worse. For neither in regard of the substance of it, nor in regard of the end of it (which is, to intend the common good) can it alter and corrupt it.

This also of Epicurus may help when you are in the most pain, that it is "neither intolerable, nor eternal" so you keep yourself to the true bounds and limits of reason and not give way to opinion.

You also must consider that there are many things which often trouble and vex you insensibly, as not armed against them with patience, because they don't ordinarily go under the name of pains, which in very deed are of the same nature as pain; as to slumber unquietly, to suffer from fever, to want appetite. When, therefore, any of these things make you discontented, check yourself with these words: Now has pain given you the foil. Your courage has failed you.

▼

Take heed lest at any time you stand so affected, though towards unnatural evil men, as ordinary men are commonly towards one another.

▼

How do we know whether Socrates was so eminent indeed, and of so extraordinary a disposition? For that he died more gloriously, that he disputed with the Sophists more subtly, that he watched in the frost more assiduously, that being commanded to fetch innocent Salaminius, he refused to do it more generously? All this will not serve.

Nor that he walked in the streets, with much gravity and majesty, as was objected to him by his adversaries, which nevertheless a man may well doubt of, whether it were so or not, or, which above all the rest, if so be that it were true, a man would well consider whether commendable, or dis-commendable. The thing therefore that we must inquire into is this: what manner of soul Socrates had. Whether his disposition was such that all that he stood upon, and sought after in this world, was barely this, that he might ever carry himself justly towards men, and in holiness towards the gods.

Neither vexing himself to no purpose at the wickedness of others, nor yet ever condescending to any man's evil fact, or evil intentions, through either fear, or engagement of friendship. Whether of those things that happened to him by God's appointment, he neither wondered at any when it happened, or thought it intolerable in the trial of it.

And lastly, whether he never did suffer his mind to sympathize with the senses, and affections of the body. For we must not think that nature has so mixed and tempered it with the body, as that she doesn't have the power to circumscribe herself, and by herself to intend her own ends and occasions.

▼

It is very possible that a man could be a very divine man and yet be altogether unknown. This you must ever be mindful of, as of this also, that a man's true happiness consists in very few things. And that although you despair that you will ever be a good either logician, or naturalist, you are never the further off by it from being either liberal, or modest, or charitable, or obedient to God.

▼

You may run out your time free from all compulsion in all cheerfulness and alacrity, though men should exclaim against you not so much, and the wild beasts should pull asunder the poor members of your pampered mass of flesh.

For what in either of these or the like cases should hinder the mind to retain her own rest and tranquility, consisting both in the right judgment of those things that happen to her, and in the ready use of all present matters and occasions? So that her judgment may say, to that which is befallen her by way of cross: this you are indeed, and according to your true nature; notwithstanding that in the judgment of opinion you appear otherwise, and her discretion to the present object you are that which I sought.

For whatever it is that is now present I shall ever embrace as a fit and seasonable object, both for my reasonable faculty and for my sociable or charitable inclination to work on.

And that which is principal in this matter, is that it may be referred either to the praise of God, or to the good of men. For either to God or to man, whatever it is that happens in the world has in the ordinary course of nature its proper reference; neither is there anything that in regard of nature is either new, or reluctant and intractable, but all things both usual and easy.

▼

A man has attained the state of perfection in his life and conversation when he so spends every day as if it were his last day, never hot and vehement in his affections, nor yet so cold and stupid as one that had no sense, and is free from all manner of dissimulation.

▼

Can the gods, who are immortal for the continuance of so many ages bear without indignation with such and so many sinners as have ever been, yes not only so, but also take such care for them that they want nothing; and do you so grievously take on as one that could bear with them no longer; you that only exist for a moment in time?

Yes, you that are one of those sinners yourself? A very ridiculous thing it is, that any man should dispense with vice and wickedness in himself, which is in his power to restrain, and should go about to suppress it in others, which is altogether impossible.

▼

Whatever object our reasonable and sociable faculty meets with that affords nothing either for the satisfaction of reason, or for the practice of charity, she worthily thinks unworthy of herself.

▼

When you have done well and another is benefited by your action, you must look like a fool if you look for a third thing besides, as that it may appear to others that you have done well, or that you may in time receive one good turn for another? No man used to be weary of that which is beneficial to him. But every action that is according to nature is beneficial. Then don't be weary of doing that which is beneficial to yourself while it is as well to others.

▼

The nature of the universe certainly did once before it was created whatever it has done since, deliberate and so resolve upon the creation of the world. Now since that time, whatever it is that is and happens in the world is either only a consequence of that one and first deliberation, or if it is that this ruling rational part of the world takes any thought and care of particular things, they are surely his reasonable and principal creatures that are the proper object of his particular care and providence. This often thought upon, is very conducive to your tranquility.

▲

Chapter Eight
They're All Dead

This also, among other things, may serve to keep you from foolish pride, if you will consider that you are now altogether incapable of the commendation of one who all his life long, or from his youth at least, has lived a philosopher's life. For both to others, and to yourself especially, it is well known that you have done many things contrary to that perfection of life.

You have therefore been confounded in your course, and from now on it will be hard for you to recover the title and credit of a philosopher. And your professional calling is repugnant to it, also[14]. Therefore if you truly understand indeed what it is that is of moment; as for your fame and credit, take no thought or care for that; let it suffice you if all the rest of your life, be it more or less, you will live as your nature requires, or according to the true and natural end of your making.

Therefore take pains to know what it is that your nature requires, and let nothing else distract you. you have already had sufficient experience, that of those many things that until now you have erred and wandered about, you could not find happiness in any of them. Not in syllogisms, and logical subtleties, not in wealth, not in honor and reputation, not in pleasure. In none of all these.

Then where is it to be found? In the practice of those things which the nature of man requires, as he is a man. How then shall he do those things? If his dogma, or moral tenets and opinions (from which all motions and actions proceed), are right and true. Which are those dogma? Those that concern that which is good or evil, as there is nothing truly good and beneficial to man but that which makes him just, temperate, courageous, and liberal; and that there is nothing truly evil and hurtful to man but that which causes the contrary effects.

▼

Whatever you do, ask yourself; How will this agree with me when it's done? Shall I have no occasion to regret it? Yet a very little while and I am dead and gone, and all things are at an end. Then what do I care for more than this, that my present action, whatever it is, may be the proper action of one that is reasonable, whose end is the common good; who in all things is ruled and governed by the same law of right and reason by which God Himself is.

▼

Alexander, Caius, Pompeius; what are these to Diogenes, Heraclitus, and Socrates? The latter penetrated into the true nature of things; into all causes, and all subjects: and upon these they exercised their power and authority. But as for the former, the extent of their error was how far their slavery extended.

▼

What they have done they will still do, even though you feel like you should hang yourself. First, don't let it trouble you. For all things both good and evil come to pass according to the nature and general condition of the universe, and within a very little while, all things will be at an end; no man will be remembered, as now of Africanus (for example) and Augustus it has already come to pass.

Then secondly, fix your mind on the thing itself; look into it, and remembering that you are bound nevertheless to be a good man, and what it is that your nature requires of you, and as you are a man, don't be diverted from what you're about, and speak that which seems to you most just; only speak it kindly, modestly, and without hypocrisy.

▼

That which the nature of the universe busies herself about is that which is here, to transfer it there, to change it, and then again to take it away, and to carry it to another place. So that you need not fear any new thing. For all things are usual and ordinary; and all things are disposed by equality.

▼

Every particular nature speeds to its content in its own proper course. A reasonable nature then speeds, when first in matter of fancies and imaginations, it gives no consent to that which is either false or uncertain.

Secondly, when in all its motions and resolutions it takes its level at the common good only, and that it desires nothing, and runs from nothing, but what is in its own power to encompass or avoid.

And lastly, when it willingly and gladly embraces whatever is dealt and appointed to it by the common nature. For it is part of it, even as the nature of any one leaf is part of the common nature of all plants and trees. But that the nature of a leaf is part of a nature both unreasonable and insensible, and which in its proper end may be hindered; or, which is servile and slavish: whereas the nature of man is part of a common nature which cannot be hindered, and which is both reasonable and just.

From where it also is, that according to the worth of everything, she makes such equal distribution of all things, as of duration, substance, form, operation, and of events and accidents. But herein don't consider whether you will find this equality in everything absolutely and by itself, but whether in all the particulars of some one thing taken together, and compared with all the particulars of some other thing, and them together likewise.

▼

You have no time nor opportunity to read? What? Don't you have time and opportunity to exercise, to not wrong yourself, to strive against all carnal pleasures and pains, to get the upper hand of them, to contemn dishonor and vainglory; and not only, to not be angry with them whom towards you you find insensible and unthankful; but also to have a care of them still, and of their welfare?

104

▼

Stop complaining about the trouble of a courtly life, either in public before others or in private by yourself.

▼

Regret is an inward and self-reprehension for the neglect or omission of something that was profitable. Now whatever is good is also profitable, and it is the part of an honest virtuous man to set by it, and to make reckoning of it accordingly. But never did any honest virtuous man regret the neglect or omission of any carnal pleasure: no carnal pleasure then is either good or profitable.

▼

What is this thing, what is it in itself, and by itself, according to its proper constitution? What is the substance of it? What is the matter, or proper use? What is the form or efficient cause? What is it for in this world, and how long will it last? This is how you must examine all things that present themselves to you.

▼

When you have a hard time waking up in the morning, remind yourself that performing actions tending to the common good is what is your own proper constitution demands, and that which the nature of man requires. But to sleep is also common to unreasonable creatures. And what more proper and natural, what more kind and pleasing, than that which is according to nature?

▼

As every fancy and imagination presents itself to you, consider, if it's be possible, the true nature and the proper qualities of it, and reason with yourself about it.

▼

At your first encounter with anyone, say presently to yourself, "What are this man's opinions concerning that which is good or evil? As concerning pain, pleasure, and the causes of both; concerning honor and dishonor, concerning life and death?" This.

Now if it is no wonder that a man should have such and such opinions, how can it be a wonder that he should do such and such things? I will remember then that he can only do as he does, holding those opinions that he does. Remember, that as it is a shame for any man to wonder that a fig tree should bear figs, so also to wonder that the world should bear anything, whatever it is which in the ordinary course of nature it may bear.

To a physician also and to a pilot it is a shame either for the one to wonder, that such and such a one should have an ague; or for the other, that the winds should prove Contrary.

▼

Remember that to change your mind upon occasion, and to follow him that is able to correct you, is equally ingenuous, as to find out at the first what is right and just without help. For nothing is required of you that is beyond the extent of your own deliberation and merit, and of your own understanding.

▼

If it were up to you to act and in your power, would you do it? If it were not, who would you then accuse? The atoms or the gods? For to do either is the part of a madman. You must therefore blame nobody, but if it is in your power, redress what is amiss; if it isn't, to what end is it to complain? For nothing should be done but to some certain end.

▼

Whatever dies and falls, however and wheresever it dies and falls, it cannot fall out of the world; here it has its abode and change, here shall it also have its dissolution into its proper elements. The same are the world's elements, and the elements of which you consist. And when they are changed, they don't murmur; why should you?

▼

Whatever anything is, it was made for something: as a horse, a vine. Why do you wonder? The sun itself will say of itself, I was made for something; and so has every god its proper function. What then were they made for? To disport and delight you? See, how even common sense and reason cannot brook it.

▼

Nature has its end as well in the end and final consummation of anything that is, as in the beginning and continuation of it.

▼

A ball is tossed in the air. Is it better going up, worse when coming down, and what if it hits the ground? So for the bubble; if it continues, is it better? And if it dissolves, is it worse? And so is it of a candle, too. So you must reason with yourself, both in matter of fame, and in matter of death.

For as for the body itself, (the subject of death) would you know the vileness of it? Turn it about that you may behold of it the worst sides, upwards as well, as in its more ordinary pleasant shape; how does it look, when it is old and withered? When sick and pained? when in the act of lust, and fornication?

And as for fame, this life is short. Both he that praises and he that is praised; he that remembers, and he that is remembered, will soon be dust and ashes. Besides, it is but in one corner of this part of the world that you are praised; and yet in this corner, you have not the joint praises of all men; no nor scarce of any one constantly. And yet the whole earth itself, what is it but as one point, in regard of the whole universe?

▼

What must be the subject of your consideration is either the matter itself, or the dogma, or the operation, or the true sense and significance.

▼

These things have happened to you most justly. Why don't you make amends? Oh, but you'd rather become good tomorrow than to be so today.

▼

Shall I do it? I will; so the end of my action is to do good to men. Should anything by way of crossness or adversity happen to me, I accept it, with reverence to the gods and their providence; the fountain of all things, from which whatever comes to pass, hangs and depends.

▼

By one action judge of the rest: this bathing which usually takes up so much of our time, what is it? Oil, sweat, filth; or the sordes of the body: an excrementitious viscosity, the excrements of oil and other ointments used about the body, and mixed with the sordes of the body: all base and loathsome. And such almost is every part of our life; and every worldly object.

▼

Lucilla buried Verus; then Lucilla herself was buried by others. So was Secunda Maximus, then Secunda herself. As well as Epitynchanus, Diotimus; then Epitynchanus himself. So Antoninus Pius, Faustina his wife; then Antoninus himself.

This is the course of the world. First Celer, Adrianus; then Adrianus himself. And those austere ones; those that foretold other men's deaths; those that were so proud and stately, where are they now? Those austere ones I mean, such as were Charax, and Demetrius the Platonic, and Eudaemon, and others like those. They were all but for one day; all dead and gone long since.

Some of them no sooner dead than forgotten. Others soon turned into fables. Of others, even that which was fabulous, is now long since forgotten. You must thereafter remember this, that whatever you are made of shall soon be dispersed, and that your life and breath, or your soul, shall either be no more or shall translated, and appointed to some certain place and station.

▼

The true joy of a man is to do that which properly belongs to man. That which is most proper to a man, is, first, to

108

be kind towards those who are of the same kind and nature as he is himself, condemning all sensual motions and appetites, discerning rightly all plausible fancies and imaginations, contemplating the nature of the universe; both it and things that are done in it.

In which kind of contemplation three several relations are to be observed: The first, to the apparent secondary cause. The Second to the first original cause, God, from whom originally proceeds whatever happens in the world. The third and last, to them that we live and converse with: what use may be made of it, to their use and benefit.

▼

If pain is evil, either it is in regard of the body; (and that cannot be, because the body of itself is altogether insensible) or in regard of the soul. But it is in the power of the soul to preserve her own peace and tranquility, and not to suppose that pain is evil. For all judgment and deliberation; all prosecution, or aversion is from within, where the sense of evil (unless it's let in by opinion) cannot penetrate.

▼

Wipe off all idle fancies, and say to yourself incessantly "Now if I will, it is in my power to keep all wickedness out of my soul; all lust, and sexual desire, all trouble and confusion.

"But on the contrary to behold and consider all things according to their true nature, and to carry myself towards everything according to its true worth." Remember then this, your power that nature has given you.

▼

Whether you speak in the Senate or whether you speak to any particular person, let your speech always be grave and modest. But you must not openly and vulgarly observe that sound and exact form of speaking, concerning that which is truly good and truly civil; the vanity of the world, and of worldly men, which otherwise truth and reason prescribes.

▼

Augustus, his court, his wife, his daughter, his nephews, his sons-in-law, his sister, Agrippa, his kinsmen, his domestics, his friends; Areus, Maecenas, his slayers of beasts for sacrifice and divination: there you have the death of a whole court together.

Proceed now on to the rest that have been since that of Augustus. Has death dwelt with them otherwise, though so many and so stately while they lived, than it does use to deal with any one particular man?

Consider now the death of a whole kindred and family, as of that of the Pompeys, as that also that used to be written upon some monuments, HE WAS THE LAST OF HIS OWN KINDRED. Oh, what care did his predecessors take, that they might leave a successor, yet behold at last one or other must of necessity be THE LAST. Here again therefore consider the death of a whole kindred.

▼

Contract your whole life to the measure and proportion of one single action. And if in every particular action you perform is fitting to the utmost of your power, let it suffice.

And who can hinder you, but that you may perform what is fitting? But there may be some outward let and impediment. Not any can hinder you, but that whatever you do, do it justly, temperately, and with the praise of God.

Yea, but there may be something, whereby some operation or other of you may be hindered. And then, with that very thing that hinders, you may he well pleased, and so by this gentle and unanimous conversion of your mind to that which may be, instead of that which at first you intended, in the room of that former action there succeeds another, which agrees as well with this contraction of your life that we now

110

speak of.

▼

Receive temporary blessings without ostentation when they are sent, and you will be able to part with them with all readiness and facility when they are taken from you again.

▼

If you ever saw either a hand, or a foot, or a head lying by itself in some place or other, as cut off from the rest of the body, such must you conceive him to make himself, as much as in him lies, that he is either offended with anything that has happened, (whatever it was) and as it were, divides himself from it: or that it commits anything against the natural law of mutual correspondence, and society among men; or, he that commits any act of uncharitableness.

Whoever you are, you are such, you are cast forth, I know not where out of the general unity, which is according to nature. You were born indeed a part, but now you have cut yourself off.

However, herein is a matter of joy and exultation, that you may be united again. God has not granted it to any other part, that once separated and cut off, it might be reunited, and come together again. But, behold, that **goodness** how great and immense it is! Which has so much esteemed **man**.

As at first he was so made, that he didn't need, except he would himself, have divided himself from the whole; so once divided and cut off, **it** has so provided and ordered it, that if he would himself, he might return, and grow together again and be admitted into its former rank and place of a part, as he was before.

▼

As almost all of her other faculties and properties, the nature of the universe has imparted to every reasonable creature, so this in particular we have received from her that as whatever opposes her, and withstands her in her purposes and intentions, though against its will and intention, she brings it about to herself to serve herself of it in the execution of her own destined ends; and so by this (though not intended) co-operation of it with herself makes it part of herself whether it will or not.

So may every reasonable creature that crosses and impedes it meets with in the course of this mortal life, it may use them as fit and proper objects to the furtherance of whatever it intended and absolutely proposed to itself as its natural end and happiness.

▼

Don't let the general representation of the wretchedness of this mortal life trouble you. Don't let your mind wander up and down, and heap together the many troubles and grievous calamities which you are as subject to as any other in her thoughts.

But as everything in particular happens, put this question to yourself, and say "What is it that in this present matter seems to you so intolerable?" For you will be ashamed to confess it.

Then upon this you should presently call to mind that neither that which is future, nor that which is past can hurt you, but that only which is present (And that also is much lessened, if you lightly circumscribe it) in her thoughts, and then check your mind if only for so little a while, (a mere instant), it cannot hold out with patience.

▼

What? Are either Panthea or Pergamus abiding to this day by their masters' tombs? Or either Chabrias or Diotimus by that of Adrianus? Oh, such tomfoolery! For what if they did, would their masters know it? Or if they knew, would they be glad of it? Or if glad, were these immortal?

Was it not also appointed to them (both men and women) to become old in time, and then to die? And these once dead, what would become of the former? And when all is done, what is all this for, but for a mere bag of blood and corruption?

▼

If you are quick-sighted, be so in matter of judgment, and best discretion, says he.

▼

In the whole constitution of man, I see no virtue contrary to justice, whereby it may be resisted and opposed. But one where pleasure and voluptuousness may be resisted and opposed, I see continence.

▼

If you can only withdraw conceit and opinion concerning that which may seem hurtful and offensive, are you yourself as safe, as safe may be? And who is that? Your reason.

"Yea, but I am not reason." Well, so be it. However, don't let your reason or understanding admit to grief, and if there is anything in you that is grieved, let that, whatever it is, conceive its own grief if it can.

▼

That which is a hindrance to the senses is an evil to your sensitive nature. That which is a hindrance of the appetitive and prosecutive faculty is an evil to your sensitive nature. As of the sensitive, so of the vegetative constitution, whatever is a hindrance to it, is also in that respect an evil to the same.

And so likewise, whatever is a hindrance to the mind and understanding must be the proper evil of the reasonable nature. Now apply all those things to yourself. Does either pain or pleasure seize on you? Let the senses look to that. Have you met with some obstacle or other in your purpose and intention? If you proposed without due reservation and exception, now has your reasonable part received a blow indeed!

But if in general you proposed to yourself whatever might be, you are not thereby either hurt, nor properly hindered. For in those things that properly belong to the mind, she cannot be hindered by any man. It is not fire, nor iron; nor the power of a tyrant, nor the power of a slandering tongue;

113

nor anything else that can penetrate into her.

▼

If once round and solid, there is no fear that ever it will change.

▼

Why should I grieve for myself, who never willingly grieved for any other? One thing rejoices one and another thing another. As for me, this is my joy, if my understanding is right and sound, as neither averse from any man, nor refusing any of those things which as a man I am subject to; if I can look on all things in the world meekly and kindly; accept all things and carry myself towards everything according to to true worth of the thing itself.

▼

Bestow upon yourself this time that is now present. They that hunt for fame after death do not consider that those men that shall be hereafter will be even such as these whom now they can so hardly bear with.

And besides they also will be mortal men. But to consider the thing in itself, if so many with so many voices, shall make such and such a sound, or shall have such and such an opinion concerning you, what is it to you?

▼

Take me and throw me where you will: I am indifferent. For there also I shall have that spirit which is within me propitious; that is, well pleased and fully contented, both in that constant disposition, and with those particular actions which to its own proper constitution are suitable and agreeable.

▼

Is this a thing of such worth that my soul should suffer for it, and become worse than it was? As either basely dejected, or inordinately affected, or confounded within itself, or terrified? What can there be that you should esteem so much?

▼

Nothing can happen to you which is not incidental to you, as you are a man. As nothing can happen either to an ox, a vine, or to a stone, which is not incidental to them; to every one in his own kind. If therefore nothing can happen to anything which is not both usual and natural, why are you displeased? Surely the common nature of all would not bring anything upon any that would be intolerable.

If, therefore, it is an external thing that causes you grief, know that it is not that properly that causes it, but your own conceit and opinion concerning the thing, which you may rid yourself of when you want. But if it is something that is amiss in your own disposition that grieves you, you may not rectify your moral tenets and opinions.

But if it grieves you that you don't perform that which seems to you right and just, why don't you choose rather to perform it than to grieve? But something that is stronger than yourself hinders you. Don't let it grieve you then, if it isn't your fault that the thing is not performed.

"Yes, but it is a thing of that nature, as that your life is not worthwhile, except it may be performed." If that is so, upon condition that you be kindly and lovingly disposed towards all men, you may be gone. For even then, as much as at any time, you are in a very good state of performance, when you die in charity with those that are an obstacle to your performance.

▼

Remember that your mind is of that nature as that it becomes altogether unconquerable, when once recalled in herself, she seeks no other content than this, that she cannot be forced. Yea, though it so falls out that it is even against reason itself that it closed handily. How much less when by the help of reason she is able to judge things with discretion?

And therefore let your chief fort and place of defense be a mind free from passions. A stronger place, (where to make his refuge, and so to become impregnable) and better fortified than this, no man has. He that doesn't see this is unlearned. He that sees it and doesn't take himself to this place of refuge is unhappy.

▼

Keep yourself to the first bare and naked apprehensions of things as they present themselves to you, and don't add to them. It is reported to you that such a one speaks ill of you. Well, he that speaks ill of you, so much is reported. But that you are hurt thereby, is not reported. That is the addition of opinion, which you must exclude.

I see that my child is sick. That he is sick, I see, but that he is in danger of his life also, I don't see. You must use this to keep yourself to the first motions and apprehensions of things as they present themselves outwardly, and don't add to them from within yourself through mere conceit and opinion. Or rather add to them, but as one that understands the true nature of all things that happen in the world.

▼

Is the cucumber bitter? Set it away. Brambles are in the way? Avoid them. Let this suffice. Don't start talking to yourself, what do these things serve for in the world? For this —one that is acquainted with the mysteries of nature will laugh at you for it, as a carpenter or a shoemaker would if meeting in either of their shops with some shavings, or small remnants of their work, you should blame them for it.

And yet those men, it is not for want of a place where to throw them that they keep them in their shops for a while, but the nature of the universe has no such out-place. Herein consists the wonder of her art and skill, that she, having once circumscribed herself within some certain bounds and limits, whatever is within her that seems either corrupted, or old, or unprofitable, she can change it into herself, and of these very things can make new things; so that she doesn't need to seek elsewhere out of herself either for a new supply of matter and substance, or for a place where to throw out whatever is irrecoverably putrid and corrupt.

Thus she, as for place, so for matter is herself sufficient to herself.

▼

Don't be slack and negligent, or loose, and wanton in your actions; nor contentious, and troublesome in your conversation; nor to rove and wander in your fancies and imaginations. Not basely to contract your soul; nor boisterously to sally out with it, or furiously to launch out as it were, nor ever to want employment.

▼

"They kill me, they cut my flesh; they persecute my person with curses." What then? May not your mind, for all this, continue pure, prudent, temperate, and just? As a fountain of sweet and clear water, though she be cursed by some bystander, yet do her springs nevertheless still run as sweet and clear as before; yea though either dirt or dung be thrown in, yet is it no sooner thrown, than dispersed, and she is cleared. She cannot be dyed or infected by it. What then must I do, that I may have within myself an overflowing fountain, and not a well? Start by continual pains and endeavors to true liberty with charity, and true simplicity and modesty.

▼

He that doesn't know what the world is doesn't know where he himself is. And he that doesn't know what the world was made for, cannot possibly know either what are the qualities, or what is the nature of the world.

Now he that in either of these is to seek, for what he himself also was made ignorant of. What then do you think of that man, who wanted for himself, as a matter of great moment, the noise and applause of men, who both where they are and what they are themselves, are altogether ignorant?

Do you desire to be commended of that man, who thrice in one hour perchance, curses himself? Do you desire to please him, who doesn't please himself? Or do you think that he pleases himself, who regrets almost everything that he does?

▼

Not only from now on to have a common breath, or to hold correspondence of breath, with that air that surrounds us; but to have a common mind, or to also hold correspondence of mind with that rational substance, which surrounds all things. For that also is of itself, and of its own nature (if a man can only draw it in as he should) everywhere diffused; and passes through all things, no less than the air does, if a man can only suck it in.

▼

Wickedness in general does not hurt the world. Particular wickedness does not hurt any other, only him it is hurtful to, whoever he is that offends, to whom in great favor and mercy it is granted, that whenever he himself shall but first desire it, he may be presently delivered of it.

To my free will my neighbor's free will, whoever he is (as his life, or his abode), is altogether indifferent. For though we are all made for one another, yet each of have our minds and understandings of them of their own proper and limited jurisdiction. For unless another man's wickedness might be my evil, which God would not have, that it might not be in another man's power to make me unhappy. That, nothing now can do but my own wickedness.

▼

The sun seems to be shed abroad. And indeed it is diffused, but not effused. For that diffusion of it is an extension. For therefore the beams of it are stretched out and extended. Now what a sunbeam is you will know if you observe the light of the sun, when through some narrow hole it pierces into some dark room it is always in a direct line.

And as with any solid body that it meets with in the way that is not penetrable by air, it is divided and abrupted, and yet neither slides off, or falls down, but stays there nevertheless. Such must the diffusion in the mind be, not an effusion, but an extension.

What obstacles and impediments she meets in her way,

she must not violently, and by way of an impetuous onset light upon them; neither must she fall down; but she must stand, and give light to that which admits it. For as for that which does not, it is its own fault and loss, if it bereaves itself of her light.

▼

He that fears death, either fears that he shall have no sense at all, or that his senses will not be the same. Whereas, he should rather comfort himself, that either no sense at all, and so no sense of evil; or if any sense, then another life, and so no death properly.

▼

All men are made one for another. Either then teach them better, or bear with them.

▼

The motion of the mind is not as the motion of a dart. For the mind when it is wary and cautious, and by way of diligent circumspection turns herself many ways, may then as well be said to go straight on to the object, as when it uses no such circumspection.

▼

Pierce and penetrate into the state of every one's understanding that you have to do with, as also to make your state open, and penetrable to any other.

▲

Chapter Nine
What Are Their Minds and Understandings?

He that is unjust is also impious. For the nature of the universe, having made all reasonable creatures for one another, to that end that they should do good to one another; more or less according to the several persons and occasions, but in no way hurt one another. It is manifest that he that transgresses against this, her will, is guilty of impiety towards the most ancient and venerable of all the deities.

For the nature of the universe is the nature the common parent of all, and therefore piously to be observed of all things that are, and that which now is, to whatever first was, and gave it its being, has relation of blood and kindred. She is also called truth and is the first cause of all truths. He therefore that willingly and wittingly lies is impious, in that he receives, and so commit injustice. He that goes against his will, in that he disagrees with the nature of the universe, and in that striving with the nature of the world he does in his particular way violate the general order of the world.

For he does no better than strive and war against it, who contrary to his own nature applies himself to that which is contrary to truth. For nature had before furnished him with instincts and opportunities sufficient for the attainment of it, which he having hereto neglected, is not now able to discern that which is false from that which is true.

He also that pursues after pleasures, as that which is truly good and flies from pains, as that which is truly evil is impious. For such a one must of necessity often accuse that common nature of distributing many things both to the evil, and to the good, not according to the deserts of either. As to the often bad pleasures, and the causes of pleasures; so to the good, pains, and the occasions of pains. Again, he that fears pains and crossness in this world, fears some of those things which some time or other must happen in the world.

And that we have already showed him to be impious.

And he that pursues after pleasures will not spare, to compass his desires, to do that which is unjust, and that is manifestly impious. Now those things which to nature are equally indifferent (for she had not created both, both pain and pleasure, if both had not been equally indifferent to her). They that will live according to nature must in those things (as being of the same mind and disposition that she is) be as equally indifferent.

Whoever therefore in either matter of pleasure and pain; death and life; honor and dishonor, (which things nature indifferently makes use of in the administration of the world) is not as indifferent, it is apparent that he is impious. When I say that common nature does indifferently make use of them, my meaning is, that they happen indifferently in the ordinary course of things, which by a necessary consequence, whether as principal or accessory, come to pass in the world, according to that first and ancient deliberation of Providence, by which she from some certain beginning resolved upon the creation of such a world, conceiving then in her womb, as it were, some certain rational generative seeds and faculties of future things, whether subjects, changes, successions; both such and such, and just so many.

▼

It would indeed be more happy and comfortable for a man to depart from this world having lived all his life long clear from all falsehood, dissimulation, voluptuousness, and pride. But if this cannot be, it is some comfort for a man to joyfully depart as weary, and out of love with those; rather than to desire to live, and to continue long in those wicked courses.

Has experience not yet taught you to fly from the plague? For a far greater plague is the corruption of the mind, than any certain change and distemper of the common air can be. This is a plague of creatures, as they are living creatures; but that of men as they are men or reasonable.

▼

You must not carry yourself scornfully in matters of death, but as one that is well pleased with it, as being one of those things that nature has appointed. For what you conceive of these, of a boy to become a young man, to wax old, to grow, to ripen, to get teeth, or a beard, or gray hair to beget, to bear, or to be delivered; or what other action it is that is natural to man according to the several seasons of his life; such a thing is it also to be dissolved.

It is therefore the part of a wise man, in matter of death, not in any way to carry himself either violently, or proudly but patiently to wait for it, as one of nature's operations: that with the same mind as now you expect when that which yet is but an embryo in your wife's belly shall come forth, you may expect also when your soul shall fall off from that outward coat or skin: wherein as a child in the belly it lies involved and shut up.

But you desire a more popular, and though not so direct and philosophical, yet a very powerful and penetrative recipe against the fear of death, nothing can make they more willing to part with your life, than if you will consider, both what the subjects themselves are that you will part with, and what manner of disposition you will no more have to do with.

It is true that you must be by no means offended with them, but take care of them, and meekly bear with them. However, this you may remember, that whenever it happens that you do depart, it shall not be from men that held the same opinions that you did. For that indeed, (if it were so) is the only thing that might make you averse to death, and willing to continue here, if it were that you are happy to live with men that had obtained the same belief that you have.

But now, what a toil it is for your to live with men of different opinions, you see: so that you have rather occasion to say, heaven, I pray you, Oh Death; lest I also in time forget myself.

▼

He that sins, sins to himself. He that is unjust, hurts himself, in that he makes himself worse than he was before. Not only that he commits, but he also that omits something, is oftentimes unjust.

▼

If my present apprehension of the object is right, and my present action charitable, and this, towards whatever proceeds from God, will be my present disposition, to be well pleased with it, It suffices.

▼

Wipe away imagination, use deliberation, quench concupiscence, keep the mind free to herself.

▼

Of all unreasonable creatures, there is but one unreasonable soul; and of all that are reasonable, but one reasonable soul, divided between them all. As of all earthly things there is but one earth, and but one light that we see by; and but one air that we breathe, as many as either breathe or see.

Now whatever partakes of some common thing, naturally affects and inclines to that whereof it is part, being of one kind and nature with it. whatever is earthly presses downwards to the common earth. whatever is liquid, would flow together. And whatever is airy, would be together likewise.

So that without some obstacle, and some kind of violence, they cannot well be kept asunder. Whatever is fiery doesn't only tend upwards by reason of the elementary fire; but here also is so ready to join, and to burn together, that whatever doesn't have sufficient moisture to make resistance is easily set on fire.

Therefore, whatever partakes of that reasonable common nature, naturally does as much and more long after his own kind. For by how much in its own nature it excels all other things, by so much more is it desirous to be joined and united to that, which is of its own nature.

As for unreasonable creatures then, they had not long been, but presently begun among them swarms, and flocks, and broods of young ones, and a kind of mutual love and affection. For though but unreasonable, these had yet a kind of soul, and therefore was that natural desire of union stronger and more intense in them than in creatures of a more excellent nature, than either in plants, or stones, or trees.

But among reasonable creatures, begun commonwealths, friendships, families, public meetings, and even in their wars, conventions, and truces. Now among them that were yet of a more excellent nature, as the stars and planets, though by their nature far distant one from another, yet even among them began some mutual correspondence and unity.

So proper is it to excellently in a high degree affect unity, as that even in things so far distant, it could operate to a mutual sympathy. But now behold what now has come to pass. Those creatures that are reasonable are now the only creatures that have forgotten their natural affection and inclination of one towards another.

Among them alone of all other things that are of one kind, there is not to be found a general disposition to flow together. But though they fly from nature, yet are they stopped in their course and apprehended. No matter what they do, nature prevails. And so will you confess, if you observe it. For you may sooner find an earthly thing where no earthly thing is than to find a man that can live by himself alone naturally.

▼

Man, God, the world, every one in their kind bears some fruits, and all things have their proper time to bear them. Though by custom, the word itself is in a manner like the vine, and the like, yet is it so nevertheless, as we have said. As for reason, that bears both common fruit for the use of others, and peculiarly, which itself enjoys. Reason is of a diffusive nature,

124

what itself is in itself, it begets in others, and so multiplies.

▼

Either teach them better if it's in your power; or if it isn't, remember that mildness and goodness was granted to you to bear with them patiently. The gods themselves are good to such. Yea and in some things, (as in matter of health, of wealth, of honor) are often content to further their endeavors, so good and gracious they are. And might you not be so, too?

Or tell me, what hinders you?

▼

Don't labor as one to whom it is appointed to be wretched, nor as one that would either be pitied or admired, but let this be your only care and desire: to always and in all things to prosecute or to forbear, as the law of charity, or mutual society requires.

▼

Today I came out of all my trouble. No, I have cast out all my trouble; it should rather be for that which troubled you, whatever it was, was not without anywhere that you should come out of it, but within in your own opinions, from where it must be cast out, before you can truly and constantly be at ease.

▼

All those things for matter of experience are usual and ordinary, for their continuance is but for a day. For their matter is most base and filthy. As they were in the days of those whom we have buried, so are they now also, and not otherwise.

▼

The things themselves that affect us stand without doors, neither knowing anything themselves nor able to utter anything to others concerning themselves. What then is it, that passes verdict on them? The understanding.

▼

As virtue and wickedness consist not in passion, but in action, so neither does the true good or evil of a reasonable charitable man consist in passion, but in operation and action.

▼

To the stone that is tossed up, when it comes down it is not hurt. Neither does it benefit when it ascends.

▼

Sift their minds and understandings, and see what men they are, whom you stand in fear of what they shall judge of you, what they themselves judge of themselves.

▼

All things that are in the world are always in a state of alteration. You also are in a perpetual change, yea and under corruption too, in some part. So is the whole world.

▼

It is not yours, but another man's sin. Why should it trouble you? Let him look to it, whose sin it is.

▼

Of an operation and of a purpose there is an ending, or of an action and of a purpose we say commonly, that it is at an end. From opinion also there is an absolute cessation, which is as it were the death of it. In all this there is no harm. Apply this now to a man's age, as first, a child; then a youth, then a young man, then an old man; every change from one age to another is a kind of death.

And all this while it is here, there is no matter of grief yet. Pass now to that life first, that which you lived under your grandfather, then under your mother, then under your father.

And thus when through the whole course of your life until now you have found and observed many alterations, many changes, many kinds of endings and cessations, put this question to yourself—what matter of grief or sorrow do you find in any of these?

Or what do you suffer through any of these? If in none of these, then neither in the ending and consummation of your whole life, which is also but a cessation and change.

▼

As occasion requires, either to your own understanding,

or to that of the universe, or to his whom you have now to do with, let your refuge be with all speed. To your own, that it resolve upon nothing against justice.

To that of the universe, that you may remember is part of who you are. Of his that you may consider whether in the state of ignorance, or of knowledge. And then also must you call to mind that he is your kinsman.

▼

As you yourself, whoever you are, were made for the perfection and consummation, being a member of it, of a common society; so must every action of yours tend to the perfection and consummation of a life that is truly sociable.

Therefore, what action of yours that either immediately or later doesn't have reference to the common good is an exorbitant and disorderly action. Yes, it is seditious, as one among the people who from such and such a consent and unity should divide and separate himself.

▼

Children's anger is mere babbling; wretched souls bearing up dead bodies, that they may not have their fall so soon: even as it is in that common dirge song.

▼

Go to the quality of the cause from which the effect proceeds. Behold it by itself bare and naked, separated from all that is material. Then consider the utmost bounds of time that that cause, thus and thus qualified, can subsist and abide.

▼

The troubles and miseries that you have already been put to are infinite, by reason of this only, because that for all happiness it did not suffice you, or that you didn't account it sufficient happiness, that your understanding operated according to its natural constitution.

▼

When any shall either impeach you with false accusations, or hatefully reproach you, or use any such carriage towards you, get presently into their minds and understandings and look in them. Behold what manner of men they are.

You will see that there is no such occasion why it should trouble you what they think of you. Yet you must love them still, for by nature they are your friends. And the gods themselves, in those things that they seek from them as matters of great moment, are well content, all manner of ways, as by dreams and oracles, to help them as well as others.

▼

Up and down, from one age to another, go the ordinary things of the world, being still the same. And either of everything in particular before it come to pass, the mind of the universe considers with itself and deliberate. If so, then submit for shame to the determination of such an excellent understanding, or once and for all it did resolve on all things in general. Since that whatever happens, happens by a necessary consequence, and all things indivisibly in a manner and inseparably hold one of another. In sum, either there is a God, and then all is well; or if all things go by chance and fortune, yet may you use your own providence in those things that concern you properly; and then are you well.

▼

Within a while the earth will cover us all, and then she herself shall have her change. And then the course will be from one period of eternity to another, and so a perpetual eternity. Now can any man that shall consider with himself in his mind the several rollings or successions of so many changes and alterations, and the swiftness of all these rulings; can he otherwise but contemn in his heart and despise all worldly things? The cause of the universe is as it were a strong torrent, it carries all away.

▼

And these your professed politicians, the only true practical philosophers of the world, (as they think of themselves) so full of affected gravity, or such professed lovers of virtue and honesty, what wretches they are indeed! How vile

128

and contemptible in themselves!

Oh, man! What ado do you keep? Do what your nature now requires. Resolve upon it, if you may, and take no thought whether anybody shall know it or not.

"Yes, but," you say, "I must not expect a Plato's commonwealth. If they profit though never so little, I must be content; and think much even of that little progress." Then do any of them forsake their former false opinions that I should think they profit?

For without a change of opinions, alas! What is all that ostentation, but mere wretchedness of slavish minds, that groan privately, and yet would make a show of obedience to reason, and truth? Go now and tell me of Alexander and Philippus, and Demetrius Phalereus. Whether they understood what the common nature requires, and could rule themselves or not, they know best themselves.

But if they kept a life, and swaggered; I (God be thanked) am not bound to imitate them. The effect of true philosophy is unaffected simplicity and modesty. Persuade me not to ostentation and vainglory.

▼

From some high place as it were to look down, and to behold here flocks, and there sacrifices without number, and all kind of navigation; some in a rough and stormy sea, and some in a calm. The general differences, or different states of things, some that are now first upon being, the several and mutual relations of those things that are together, and some other things that are at their last.

Their lives also, who were long ago, and theirs who shall be hereafter, and the present state and life of those many nations of barbarians that are now in the world, you must likewise consider in your mind. And how many there are who never so much as heard of your name, how many that will soon forget it; how many who but even now commended you, within a very little while perchance will speak ill of you.

So that neither fame, nor honor, nor anything else that

this world affords is worth the while. The sum then of all; whatever happens to you, whereof God is the cause, to accept it contentedly. Whatever you do, whereof you yourself are the cause, to do it justly, which will be, if both in your resolution and in your action you have no further end than to do good to others, as being that, which by your natural constitution as a man, you are bound to.

▼

It is in your power to cut off many of those things that trouble and narrow you, as wholly depending from mere conceit and opinion, and then you will have room enough.

▼

Comprehend the whole world together in your mind, and the whole course of this present age to represent it to yourself, and to fix your thoughts upon the sudden change of every particular object. How short the time is from the generation of anything to its dissolution; but how immense and infinite both that which was before the generation, and that which after the generation it will be.

Everything that you see will soon perish, and they that see their corruption will soon vanish themselves. He that dies at a hundred years old, and he that dies young, shall come all to one.

▼

What are their minds and understandings, and the things that they apply themselves to? What do they love, and what do they hate?

Fancy to yourself the state of their souls to be openly seen. When they think they hurt them shrewdly whom they speak ill of, and when they think they do them a very good turn whom they commend and extol, oh, how full are they then of conceit, and opinion!

▼

Loss and corruption is indeed nothing else but change and alteration; and that is it which the nature of the universe most delights in, by which, and according to which, whatever is done is done well. For that was the state of worldly things from the beginning, and so shall it ever be.

Or would you rather say that all things in the world have gone ill from the beginning for so many ages, and shall ever go ill? And then among so many deities, could no divine power be found all this while that could rectify the things of the world? Or is the world forever condemned to incessant woes and miseries?

▼

How base and putrid every common matter is! Water, dust, and bones from the mixture of these, and all that loathsome stuff that our bodies consist of; so subject to be infected and corrupted.

And again those other things that are so much prized and admired, as marble stones, what are they but the kernels of the earth? Gold and silver, what are they, but as the more gross feces of the earth?[15] Your most royal apparel, for matter, it is but as it were the hair of a silly sheep, and for color, the very blood of a shellfish; of this nature are all other things.

Your life itself is some such thing too; a mere exhalation of blood, and it also is apt to be changed into some other common thing.[*]

▼

Will this querulousness, this murmuring, this complaining and dissembling never be at an end? What is it then that troubles you? Does any new thing happen to you? What do you so wonder at, at the cause, or the matter?

Behold either by itself, is either of that weight and moment indeed? And besides these, there is nothing. But your duty towards the gods also, it is time you should acquit yourself of it with more goodness and simplicity.

▼

It is all one thing to see these things for a hundred years together, or but for three years.

▼

If he has sinned, his is the harm, not mine. But

131

perchance he has not.

▼

Either all things by the providence of reason happen to every particular as a part of one general body, and then it is against reason that a part should complain of anything that happens for the good of the whole; or if, according to Epicurus, atoms are the cause of all things and that life is nothing else but an accidental confusion of things, and death nothing else but a mere dispersion and so of all other things, what do you trouble yourself for?

▼

Do you say to that rational part, "you are dead; corruption has taken hold of you?" Does it then also void excrement? Does it, like either oxen or sheep, graze or feed; that it also should be mortal, as well as the body?

▼

Either the gods can do nothing for us at all, or they can still and allay all the distractions and annoyances of your mind. If they can do nothing, why do you pray? If they can, why would you not rather pray that they will grant to you that you may neither fear, nor lust after any of those worldly things which cause these distractions and annoyances of it?

Why not, rather, that you may not be grieved and discontented at either their absence or presence, than either that you may obtain them, or that you may avoid them? For certainly it must be that if the gods can help us in anything, they may in this kind also.

But you will say perchance, "In those things the gods have given me my liberty, and it is in my own power to do what I will." But if you may use this liberty, rather to set your mind at true liberty, than willfully with baseness and servility of mind to affect those things which either to compass or to avoid is not in your power, were you not better?

And as for the gods, who have told you that they may not help us up even in those things that they have put in our own power? Whether it be so or not, you will soon perceive if you will only try yourself and pray.

One prays that he may compass his desire, to lie with such or such a one, you pray that you may not lust to lie with her. Another how he may be rid of such a one; pray that you may so patiently bear with him, as that you have no such need to be rid of him.

Another, that he may not lose his child. Pray you that you may not fear to lose him. To this end and purpose, let all your prayers be, and see what will be the event.

▼

"In my sickness," says Epicurus of himself, "my discourses were not concerning the nature of my disease, neither was that, to them that came to visit me, the subject of my talk. In the consideration and contemplation of that which was of special weight and moment was all my time bestowed and spent, and among others in this very thing, how my mind, by a natural and unavoidable sympathy partaking in some sort with the present indisposition of my body, might nevertheless keep herself free from trouble, and in present possession of her own proper happiness.

"Neither did I leave the ordering of my body to the physicians altogether to do with me what they would, as though I expected any great matter from them, or as though I thought it a matter of such great consequence, by their means to recover my health.

"For my present state, I thought, liked me very well, and gave me good content." Whether therefore in sickness (if you chance to sicken) or in whatever other kind of extremity, endeavor also to be in your mind so affected, as he reports of himself. Not to depart from your philosophy for anything that can befall you, nor to give ear to the discourses of silly people, and mere naturalists.

▼

It is common to all trades and professions to mind and intend only that which now they are about, and the instruments they work with.

▼

When at any time you are offended with any one's impudence, put this question to yourself: "What? Is it then possible that there should not be any impudent men in the world?! Certainly it is not possible."

Don't desire, then, that which is impossible. For this one, (you must think) whoever he is, is one of those impudent ones that the world cannot be without. So of the subtle and crafty, so of the perfidious, so of every one that offends, must you ever be ready to reason with yourself.

For while in general you reason like that with yourself, that the kind of them must be in the world, you will be the better able to use meekness towards every particular one. You will also will find of very good use, upon every such occasion, presently to consider with yourself what proper virtue nature has furnished man with against such a vice, or to encounter with a disposition vicious in this kind.

As for example, against the unthankful, it has given goodness and meekness as an antidote, and so against another vicious in another kind some other peculiar faculty. And generally, isn't it in your power to instruct him better, that he is in an error?

For whoever sins, does in that decline from his purposed end, and is certainly deceived. And again, what are you the worse for his sin? For you will not find that any one of these against whom you are incensed has in very deed done anything whereby your mind (the only true subject of your hurt and evil) can be made worse than it was.

And what a matter of either grief or wonder is this, if he that is unlearned, do the deeds of one that is unlearned? Shouldn't you rather blame yourself, who, when upon very good grounds of reason, you might have thought it very probable that such a thing would by such a one be committed, did not only not foresee it, but moreover wonder at it, that such a thing should be.

But then especially, when you find fault with either an unthankful, or a false man, must you reflect upon yourself. For without all question, you yourself are much in fault, if either of one that were of such a disposition, you expected that he should be true to you. Or when to any you did a good turn, you did not there bound your thoughts as one that had obtained his end; nor did not think that from the action itself you had received a full reward of the good that you had done. For what would you have more?

To him that is a man, you have done a good turn. Does that not suffice you? What your nature required, that you have done. Must you be rewarded for it? As if either the eye for that it sees, or the feet that they go, should require satisfaction.

For as these being by nature appointed for such a use, can challenge no more than that they may work according to their natural constitution. So man being born to do good to others whensoever he does a real good to any by helping them out of error; or though but in middle things, as in matter of wealth, life, preferment, and the like, helps to further their desire that he does that for which he was made, and therefore can require no more.

▲

Chapter Ten
Serve What Is In Your Nature

Oh, my soul, I trust the time will be when you will be good, simple, single, more open and visible, than that body by which it is enclosed. You will one day be sensible of their happiness, whose end is love, and their affections dead to all worldly things. You will one day be full, and in want of no external thing—not seeking pleasure from anything, either living or insensible, that this world can afford; neither wanting time for the continuation of your pleasure, nor place and opportunity, nor the favor either of the weather or of men.

When you will be content with your present state, and all things present shall add to your contentment; when you will persuade yourself that you have all things, all for your good, and all by the providence of the gods.

Of future things will also be as confident that all will do well, as tending to the maintenance and preservation in some sort, of his perfect welfare and happiness, who is perfection of life, of goodness, and beauty; who begets all things, and contains all things in himself, and in himself remembers all things from all places that are dissolved, that of them he may beget others again like to them.

Such one day shall be your disposition, that you will be able, both in regard of the gods, and in regard of men, so to fit and order your conversation as neither to complain of them at any time, for anything that they do; nor to do anything yourself, for which you may justly be condemned.

▼

As one who is altogether governed by nature, let it be your care to serve what it is that your nature in general requires. That done, if you don't find that your nature will be the worse for it, as you are a living sensible creature, you may proceed.

Next, then, you must examine what your nature is, as you are a living sensible creature, requires. And that, whatever it is, you may admit of and do it, if your nature as you are a reasonable living creature will not be the worse for it.

Now whatever is reasonable is also sociable. Keep yourself to these rules, and don't trouble yourself about idle things.

▼

Whatever happens to you, you with your natural constitution are either able, or not able to bear it. If you are able, don't be offended, but bear it according to your natural constitution, or as nature has enabled you.

If you are not able, don't be offended. For it will soon make an end of you, and itself, (whatever it is) at the same time. But remember, that whatever by the strength of opinion, grounded upon a certain apprehension of both true profit and duty, you can conceive tolerability; that you are able to bear that by your natural constitution.

▼

Teach with love and meekness to him that offends, and to show him his error. But if you can't, then to blame yourself; or rather not blame yourself, if your will and endeavors have not been wanting.

▼

Whatever it is that happens to you, it is that which was appointed to you from all time. For by the same coherence of causes, by which your substance from all eternity was appointed to be, was also whatever should happen to it destined and appointed.

▼

Either with Epicurus, we must fondly imagine the atoms to be the cause of all things, or we must grant a nature. Let this then be your first ground, that you are part of that universe which is governed by nature.

Then secondly, that to those parts that are of the same kind and nature as you are, you have relation of kindred. For of these, if I shall always be mindful, first as I am a part, I shall never be displeased with anything that falls to my particular share of the common chances of the world.

For nothing that is needful to the whole can be truly hurtful to that which is part of it. For this being the common privilege of all natures, that they contain nothing in themselves that is harmful to them; it cannot be that the nature of the universe (whose privilege beyond other particular natures is that she cannot be constrained against her will by any higher external cause) should beget anything and cherish it in her bosom that should tend to her own hurt and prejudice.

As then I bear in mind that I am a part of such a universe, I shall not be displeased with anything that happens. And as I have relation of kindred to those parts that are of the same kind and nature that I am, so I shall be careful to do nothing that is prejudicial to the community, but in all my deliberations they that are of my kind shall ever be. The common good, that which all my intentions and resolutions shall drive to, as that which is contrary to it, I shall by all means endeavor to prevent and avoid.

These things once so fixed and concluded, as you would think him a happy citizen, whose constant study and practice were for the good and benefit of his fellow citizens, and the carriage of the city such towards him, that he were well pleased with it; so must it be with you, that you will live a happy life.

▼

All parts of the world (I mean things that are contained within the whole world) must of necessity at some time or other come to corruption. Alteration I should say, to speak truly and properly, but that I may be the better understood, I am content at this time to use that more common word.

Now I say, if it is that this is both hurtful to them, and yet unavoidable, wouldn't the whole itself be in a sweet case, all the parts of it being subject to alteration? Yes, and by their making itself fitted for corruption, as consisting of things different and contrary?

And did nature then either of herself thus project and purpose the affliction and misery of her parts, and therefore made them of a purpose, not only that by chance they might, but of necessity that they should fall into evil; or did she not know what she did when she made them? For to say either of these two is equally absurd.

But to let pass nature in general, and to reason of things particularly according to their own particular natures, how absurd and ridiculous it is, first to say that all parts of the whole are, by their proper natural constitution, subject to alteration; and then when any such thing happens, as when one falls sick and dies, to take on and wonder as though some strange thing had happened?

Though this besides might not move so grievously as to take on when any such thing happens, that whatever is dissolved, it is dissolved into those things it was compounded from. For every dissolution is either a mere dispersion of the elements into those elements again how everything consisted, or a change, of that which is more solid into earth, and of that which is pure and subtle or spiritual, into air.

So that by this means nothing is lost, but all resumed again into those rational generative seeds of the universe; and this universe, either after a certain period of time to lie consumed by fire, or by continual changes to be renewed, and so forever to endure.

Now that solid and spiritual that we speak of, you must not conceive it to be that very same, which at first was, when you were born. For alas! All this that now you are in either kind, either for a matter of substance, or of life, was but two or three days ago partly from meats that were eaten, and partly from air breathed in, received all its influx, being the same then in no other respect than a running river, maintained by the perpetual influx and new supply of waters, is the same.

That, therefore, which you have since received, not that which came from your mother, is that which comes to change and corruption.

But suppose that that for the general substance, and more solid part of it, should still cleave to you never so close, yet what is that to the proper qualities and affections of it, by which persons are distinguished, which certainly are quite different?

▼

Now that you have seen that these names are good, modest, true; of emfrwn, sumfrwn, uperfrwn; take heed lest at any time by doing anything that is contrary to you but so-called improperly, you lose your right to these appellations. Or if you do, return to them again with all possible speed.

And remember, that the word *emfrwn* notes to you an intent and intelligent consideration of every object that presents itself to you without distraction. And the word *emfrwn* is a ready and contented acceptation of whatever by the appointment of the common nature happens to you.

And the word *sumfrwn*, a super-extension, or a transcendent, and outreaching disposition of your mind, whereby it passes by all bodily pains and pleasures, honor and credit, death and whatever is of the same nature, as matters of absolute indifference, and in no way to be stood upon by a wise man.

These, then, you will observe, if inviolably, and will not be ambitious to be so called by others, both you yourself will become a new man, and you will begin a new life. For to continue such as you have been before, to undergo those distractions and annoyances as you need for such a life as you have lived so far, is the part of one that is very foolish, and is overfond of his life, whom a man might compare to one of those half-eaten wretches, matched in the amphitheater with wild beasts; who as full as they are all the body over with wounds and blood, desire for a great favor that they may be reserved till the next day, then also, and in the same state to be exposed to the same nails and teeth as before.

Therefore, ship yourself away, and from the troubles and distractions of your former life convey yourself as it were to these few names. If you can abide in them, or be constant in the practice and possession of them, continue there as glad and joyful as one that was translated to some such place of bliss and happiness as that which by Hesiod and Plato is called the Islands of the Blessed, by others called the Elysian Fields.

And whenever you find yourself in danger of a relapse, and that you are not able to master and overcome those difficulties and temptations that present themselves in your present station, get into any private corner where you may be better able. Or if that will not serve, rather forsake even your life.

But do it so that it be not in passion but in a plain voluntary modest way, this being the only commendable action of your whole life since you have departed, or this having been the main work and business of your whole life, that you might thus depart.

Now for the better remembrance of those names that we have spoken of, you will find it a very good help to remember the gods as often as may be, and that the thing which they require at our hands of as many of us, as are by nature reasonable creation is not that with fair words, and outward show of piety and devotion we should flatter them, but that we should become like them.

That is as all other natural creatures, the fig tree for example; the dog, the bee: both do, all of them, and apply themselves to that which by their natural constitution is proper to them. So man should do that likewise, which by his nature, as he is a man, belongs to him.

▼

Toys and fooleries at home, wars abroad; sometimes terror, sometimes torpor, or stupid sloth—this is your daily slavery. Little by little, if you don't look to it better, those sacred dogma will be blotted out of your mind. How many things are there which, when as a mere naturalist, you had barely considered according to their nature, you let pass without any further use?

Whereas you should in all things join in action and contemplation, that you might both at the same time attend all present occasions, to perform everything duly and carefully, and yet so intend the contemplative part too, that no part of that delight and pleasure, which the contemplative knowledge of everything according to its true nature affords itself might be lost.

Or, that the true and contemplative knowledge of everything according to its own nature, might of itself, (action being subject to many lets and impediments) afford to you sufficient pleasure and happiness. Not apparent indeed, but not concealed.

And when will you attain to the happiness of true simplicity, and unaffected gravity? When will you rejoice in the certain knowledge of every particular object according to its true nature, as what the matter and substance of it is. What use it is for in the world, how long it can subsist, what things it consists of. Who they are that are capable of it, and who they are that can give it and take it away?

▼

As the spider, when it has caught the fly that it hunted, is not proud, nor meanly conceited of herself, as he likewise that has caught a hare, or has taken a fish with his net, another for the taking of a boar, and another of a bear; so may they be proud, and applaud themselves for their valiant acts against the *Sarmatai*, or northern nations lately defeated.

For these also, these famous soldiers and warlike men, if you look into their minds and opinions, what do they do for the most part but hunt after prey?

▼

Find out, and set to yourself some certain way and method of contemplation whereby you may clearly discern and represent to yourself the mutual change of all things, the one into the other. Bear it in mind forever, and see that you are thoroughly well exercised in this particular matter. For there is not anything more effectual to beget true magnanimity.

▼

He has gotten loose from the bonds of his body, and perceiving that within a very little while he must of necessity bid the world farewell, and leave all these things behind him, he wholly applied himself as to righteousness in all his actions, so to the common nature in all things that should happen to him.

And contenting himself with these two things, to do all things justly, and whatever God sends to like well of it, what others shall either say or think of him, or shall do against him, he does not so much as trouble his thoughts with it.

To go on straight, whether right and reason directed him, and by so doing to follow God, was the only thing that he minded, his only business and occupation.

▼

What use is there of suspicion at all? Or, why should thoughts of mistrust, and suspicion concerning that which is in the future trouble your mind at all? What now is to be done, if you may search and inquire into that, what do you care for more?

And if you are well able to perceive it alone, let no man divert you from it. But if alone you don't perceive it so well, suspend your action and take advice from the best.

And if there is anything else that hinders you, go on with prudence and discretion, according to the present occasion and opportunity, still proposing that to yourself which you conceive most right and just. For to hit that aright, and to speed in the prosecution of it must be happiness, since it is that only which we can truly and properly be said to miss of, or miscarry in.

▼

What is that that is slow, and yet quick? Merry, and yet grave? He that follows reason in all things for his guide.

▼

In the morning as soon as you wake up, before either

143

your affections, or external objects have wrought upon your judgment, it is yet most free and impartial. Put this question to yourself, whether if that which is right and just be done, the doing of it by yourself, or by others when you are not able yourself is a material thing or not.

For sure it is not. And as for these that keep such a life, and stand so much upon the praises, or dispraises of other men, have you forgotten what manner of men they are? That such and such upon their beds, and such at their board, what their ordinary actions are, what they pursue after, and what they fly from? What thefts and rapes they commit, if not with their hands and feet, yet with that more precious part of them, their minds, which (would it but admit of them) might enjoy faith, modesty, truth, justice, a good spirit?

▼

"Give what you will, and take away what you will," says he that is well taught and truly modest, to him that gives and takes away. And it is not out of a stout and peremptory resolution, that he says it, but in mere love and humble submission.

▼

So live as indifferent to the world and all worldly objects, as one who lives by himself on some desert hill. For whether here, or there, if the whole world is but as one town, it matters not much for the place.

Let them behold and see a man that is a man indeed, living according to the true nature of man. If they cannot bear with me, let them kill me. For better were it to die, than so to live as they would have you.

▼

Don't make it a matter of dispute or discourse any longer, what the signs and proprieties of a good man are, but to really and actually be such.

Always represent to yourself, and to set before you, both the general age and time of the world, and the whole substance of it. And how all things in particular, respect these as for their substance, as one of the least seeds that is, and for their duration, as the turning of the pestle in the mortar once about.

Then to fix your mind on every particular object of the world, and to conceive it as it really is, as already being in the state of dissolution, and of change; tending to some kind of either putrefaction or dispersion, or whatever else it is that is the death, as it were, of everything in his own kind.

▼

Consider them through all actions and occupations, of their lives: as when they eat, and when they sleep. When they are in the act of necessary exoneration, and when in the act of lust. Again, when they either are in their greatest exultation, and in the middle of all their pomp and glory, or being angry and displeased, in great state and majesty, as from an higher place, they chide and rebuke.

How base and slavish, but a little while ago, they were fain to be, that they might come to this, and within a very little while what will be their state when death has once seized them.

▼

It is best for every one that the common nature of all sends to every one, and then it is best when she sends it.

▼

"The earth," says the poet, "often longs after the rain. So is the glorious sky often as desirous to fall upon the earth, which argues a mutual kind of love between them." And so, I say, does the world bear a certain affection of love to whatever shall come to pass with your affections shall I concur, Oh, world.

The same (and no other) shall the object of my longing, is which is of yours. Now that the world's love is true indeed, so is it as commonly said and acknowledged, when according to the Greek phrase, imitated by the Latins, of things that used to be, we say commonly that they love to be.

▼

Either you continue in this kind of life and what it is, which for so long you have been used to it and therefore tolerable, or you retire, or leave the world, and that of your own accord, and then you have your mind: or your life is cut off; and then may you rejoice that you have ended your charge. One of these must be. Be therefore of good comfort.

▼

Let it always appear and be manifest to you that solitariness, and desert places, so much esteemed of and affected by many philosophers, are of themselves but thus and thus; and that all things are them to them that live in towns, and converse with others as they are the same nature everywhere to be seen and observed.

To them that have retired themselves to the top of mountains, and to desert havens, or what other desert and inhabited places. For you will find it anywhere and you may quickly find and apply that to yourself which Plato said of his philosopher, in a place: "As private and retired," says he, "as if he were shut up and enclosed about in some shepherd's lodge, on the top of a hill."

Put these questions there by yourself, or to enter in these considerations: what is the chief and principal part which has power over the rest? What is now the present state of it, as I use it? What is it that I employ it about? Is it now void of reason or not? Is it free, and separated; or so affixed, so congealed and grown together as it were with the flesh, that it is swayed by the motions and inclinations of it?

▼

Someone who runs away from his master is a fugitive. But the law is every man's master. Therefore, anyone who forsakes the law is a fugitive.

So is anyone, whoever they are, who is either sorry,

angry, or afraid, or for anything that either has been, is, or shall be by his appointment, who is the Lord and Governor of the universe.

For he truly and properly is *Nomoz*, or the law, as the distributor and dispenser of all things that happen to anyone in his lifetime. Whoever, then, is either sorry, angry, or afraid is a fugitive.

▼

From man is the seed, that once cast into the womb he has nothing more to do with. Another cause succeeds, and undertakes the work, and in time brings a child (that wonderful effect from such a beginning!) to perfection.

Again, man lets food down through his throat; and that once down, he has no more to do with it. Another cause succeeds and distributes this food into the senses, and the affections. Into life, and into strength, and does with it those other many and marvelous things that belong to man.

These things therefore that are so secretly and invisibly wrought and brought to pass, you must use to behold and contemplate, not the things themselves only, but the power also by which they are affected, that you may behold it, though not with the eyes of the body, yet as plainly and visibly as you can see and discern the outward efficient cause of the depression and elevation of anything.

▼

Always keep in mind and consider how all things that now are, have been much after the same sort, and after the same fashion that they now are. So think of those things which shall be hereafter as well.

Moreover, whole drama, and uniform scenes, or scenes that comprehend the lives and actions of men of one calling and profession, as many as either in your own experience you have known, or by reading of ancient histories (as the whole court of Adrianus, the whole court of Antoninus Pius, the whole court of Philippus, that of Alexander, that of Croesus) to set them all before your eyes. For you will find that they are all

147

but after one sort and fashion, only that the actors were others.

▼

As a pig that cries and flings when his throat is cut, fancy to yourself every one to is that grieves for any worldly thing. Such a one is he also who, upon his bed alone, bewails the miseries of this, our mortal life.

And remember this, that only to reasonable creatures is it granted that they may willingly and freely submit to Providence, but absolutely to submit is a necessity imposed upon all creatures equally.

▼

Whatever it is that you go about, consider it yourself and ask yourself, "What? because I shall do this no more when I am dead, should therefore death seem grievous to me?"

▼

When you are offended with any man's transgression, presently reflect on yourself, and consider what you yourself are guilty of in the same kind. As that you also maybe think it a happiness either to be rich, or to live in pleasure, or to be praised and commended, and so of the rest in particular.

For if you will call this to mind, you will soon forget your anger; especially when at the same time this also shall concur in your thoughts, that he was constrained by his error and ignorance, for how can he choose as long as he is of that opinion? Therefore if you can, take that away from him that forces him to do as he does.

▼

When you see Satyro, think of Socraticus and Eutyches, or Hymen. When Euphrates, think of Eutychio, and Sylvanus. When Alciphron, of Tropaeophorus, when Xenophon, of Crito, or Severus.

And when you look upon yourself, fancy to yourself some one or other of the Caesars; and so for every one, some one or other that has been answerable for state and profession to him.

Then let this come to your mind at the same time; and where now are they all? Nowhere or anywhere? For so will you at all time be able to perceive how all worldly things are like the smoke that vanishes away, or indeed, mere nothing.

Especially when you will call this to mind also, that whatever is once changed, shall never be again as long as the world endures. And you then, how long will you endure? And why does it not suffice you, if virtuously, and as becomes you, you may pass that portion of time, how little it may be, that is allotted to you?

▼

What a subject, and what a course of life it is, that you so much desire to be rid of. For all these things, what are they but fit objects for an understanding, that beholds everything according to its true nature, to exercise itself upon?

Be patient, therefore, until that (as a strong stomach that turns all things into his own nature; and as a great fire that turns in flame and light whatever you cast into it) you have made these things also familiar, and as it were, natural to you.

▼

Don't let it be in any man's power to truthfully say that you are not truly simple, or sincere and open, or not good. Let whoever he is that shall have any such opinion of you be deceived. For all this depends on you.

Who is it that should hinder you from being either truly simple or good? Do you only resolve rather not to live, than not to be such? For indeed neither does it stand with reason that he should live that is not such.

What then is it that may upon this present occasion according to best reason and discretion, either be said or done? For whatever it is, it is in your power either to do it, or to say it, and therefore seek not any pretenses, as though you were hindered. You will never cease groaning and complaining until such time as what pleasure is to the voluptuous will be to you, to do in everything that presents itself, whatever may be done comfortably and agreeably to the proper constitution of man, or, to man as he is a man.

For you must account that pleasure, whatever it is, that you may do according to your own nature. And to do this, every place will fit you, to the cylinders, or rollers, it is not granted to move everywhere according to its own proper motion, as neither to the water, nor to the fire, nor to any other thing that either is merely natural, or natural and sensitive, but not rational for many things there be that can hinder their operations.

But of the mind and understanding this is the proper privilege, that according to its own nature, and as it will itself, it can pass through every obstacle that it finds, and keep straight on forwards. Setting therefore before your eyes this happiness and felicity of your mind, whereby it is able to pass through all things, and is capable of all motions, whether as the fire, upwards; or as the stone downwards, or as the cylinders through that which is sloping: content yourself with it, and don't seek any other thing.

For all other kinds of hindrances that are not hindrances of your mind, either they are proper to the body, or merely proceed from the opinion, reason not making that resistance that it should, but basely, and cowardly suffering itself to be foiled. Of themselves they can neither wound, nor do any hurt at all. Else must he of necessity, whoever he is that meets with any of them, become worse than he was before.

For so is it in all other subjects, that that is thought hurtful to them where they are made worse. But here contrariwise, man (if he make that good use of them that he should) is rather the better and the more praiseworthy for any of those kind of hindrances than otherwise.

But generally remember that nothing can hurt a natural citizen that is not hurtful to the city itself, nor anything hurt the city that is not hurtful to the law itself. But none of these casualties, or external hindrances, hurt the law itself; or, are contrary to that course of justice and equity, by which public societies are maintained. Neither, therefore, do they hurt either city or citizen.

▼

As he that is bitten by a rabid dog is afraid of almost everything that he sees, so to him whom the dogma have once bitten, or in whom true knowledge has made an impression, everything almost that he sees or reads be it never so short or ordinary, affords a good memento; to put him out of all grief and fear, as that of the poet, "The winds blow upon the trees, and their leaves fall upon the ground.

"Then do the trees begin to bud again, and by the springtime they put forth new branches. So is the generation of men; some come into the world, and others go out of it." Of these leaves then your children are.

And also they that applaud you so gravely, or, that applaud your speeches, with that their usual acclamation "*axiopistwz*"; "Oh, I am wisely spoken and speak well of you," as on the other side they that don't stick to your curse, they that privately and secretly dispraise and deride you, they are also only leaves.

And they also that shall follow, in whose memories the names of men who were famous after death is preserved, they are but leaves either. For it is even of all these worldly things. Their spring comes, and they are put forth. Then blows the wind, and they go down.

And then in lieu of them grow others out of the wood or common matter of all things, like to them. But to endure but for a while is common to all. Then why should you so earnestly either seek after these things, or flee from them, as though they should endure for ever? Yet a little while and your eyes will be closed up, and for him that carries you to your grave shall mourn for another within a while after.

▼

A good eye must be good to see whatever is to be seen, and not just pleasant things only. For that is proper to sore eyes. So must a good ear, and a good smell be ready for whatever it is

151

either to be heard, or smelled, and a good stomach as indifferent to all kinds of food as a millstone is to whatever it was made to grind.

Therefore, a sound understanding must be ready for whatever happens. But he that says, "Oh, that my children might live!" And "oh, that all men might commend me for whatever I do!" is an eye that seeks after pleasant things, or as teeth wanting that which is tender.

▼

There is not any man that is so happy in his death but that some of those that are by him when he dies will be ready to rejoice at his supposed calamity. Is it one that was virtuous and wise indeed?

Will there not be some one or other that is found who will say to himself; "Well now at last shall I be at rest from this pedagogue. He did not indeed otherwise trouble us much, but I know well enough that in his heart, he condemned us much."

Thus will they speak of the virtuous. But as for us, alas! How many things are there for which there are many that would be glad to be rid of us. This, therefore, if you will think of whenever you die, you will die the more willingly, When you will think with yourself "I am now to depart from that world, wherein those that have been my nearest friends and acquaintances, they whom I have so much suffered for, so often prayed for, and for whom I have taken such care, even they would have me die, hoping that after my death they shall live happier than they did before."

Why then should any man desire to continue here any longer? Nevertheless, whenever you die, you must not be less kind and loving to them for it; but as before, see them, continue to be their friend, to wish them well, and meekly, and gently to carry yourself towards them, but yet so that on the other side, it will not make you the more unwilling to die.

But as it fares with them that die an easy, quick death, whose soul is soon separated from their bodies, so must your separation from them be. To these had nature joined and annexed me, now she parts us. I am ready to depart, as from friends and kinsmen, but yet without either hesitation or compulsion. For this is also according to Nature.

▼

Use yourself as often as whenever you see any man do anything, presently, if it's possible, to say to yourself, "What is this man's end in this his action?" But begin this course with yourself first of all, and diligently examine yourself concerning whatever you do.

▼

Remember that whatever sets a man at work and has power over the affections to draw them either one way or the other is not properly any external thing, but that which is hidden within every man's dogma and opinions. That which is rhetoric, that is life; that (to speak truly) is man himself.

As for your body, which as a vessel, or a case, compasses you about, and the many and curious instruments that it has annexed to it, let them not trouble your thoughts. For of themselves they are but as a carpenter's ax, but that they are born with us, and naturally sticking to us.

But otherwise, without the inward cause that has power to move them, and to restrain them, those parts are of themselves of no more use to us than the shuttle is of itself to the weaver, or the pen to the writer, or the whip to the coachman.

▲

Chapter Eleven
The Privileges of a Reasonable Soul

The natural properties and privileges of a reasonable soul are that she sees that she can order and compose herself, that she makes herself however she wants, that she reaps her own fruits, whereas plants, trees, unreasonable creatures, whatever fruit (whether proper fruit or analogically only) they bear, they bear them to others, and not to themselves.

Again, whenever and wherever, sooner or later, her life will end, she has her own end nevertheless. For it is not with her, as with dancers and players, who if they are interrupted in any part of their action, the whole action must be imperfect. She in whatever part of time or action she is surprised, can make that which she has in her hand, whatever it is, complete and full, so that she may depart with that comfort.

"I have lived; neither want I anything of that which properly belonged to me." Again, she compasses the whole world, and penetrates into the vanity, and mere outside (wanting substance and solidity) of it, and stretches herself to the infinity of eternity. The revolution or restoration of all things after a certain period of time to the same state and place as before, she fetches about and comprehends in herself.

She also considers in addition, and sees clearly that neither they that shall follow us will see any new thing that we have not seen, nor they that went before anything more than we, but that he that is once come to forty (if he has any wit at all) can in a manner (for that they are all of one kind) see all things, both past and future.

As proper is it, and natural to the soul of man to love her neighbor, to be true and modest; and to regard nothing so much as herself, which is also the property of the law. Whereby by the way it appears that sound reason and justice comes all to one, and therefore that justice is the chief thing that reasonable creatures ought to propose to themselves as their end.

A pleasant song or dance; the Pancratiast's exercise, sports that you would to be much taken with, you will easily contemn. If you will divide the harmonious voice into so many particular sounds it consists of, and of every one in particular, you shall ask yourself whether this or that sound it is that it conquers you. For you will be ashamed of it.

And so for shame, if accordingly you will consider every particular motion and posture by itself. So for the wrestler's exercise, too. Generally then, whatever it is besides virtue and those things that proceed from virtue that you are subject to be much affected with, remember presently to divide it, and by this kind of division, in each particular to attain to the contempt of the whole.

This you must transfer and apply to your whole life also.

▼

That soul which is ever ready, even now if need be, to leave the body, whether by way of extinction, or dispersion, or continuation in another place and state to be separated, how blessed and happy is it!

But this readiness of it must proceed, not from an obstinate and peremptory resolution of the mind, violently and passionately set upon opposition, as Christians usually are, but from a peculiar judgment, with discretion and gravity, so that others may be also persuaded and drawn to the example, but without any noise and passionate exclamations.

▼

Have I done anything charitably? Then I have benefited from it. See that upon all occasions this may present itself to your mind, and never cease to think about it.

What is your profession? To be good. And how should this be well brought to pass, but by certain theorems and doctrines, some concerning the nature of the universe, and some concerning the proper and particular constitution of man?

▼

Tragedies were at first brought in and instituted to put men in mind of worldly chances and casualties. These things in the ordinary course of nature happened that men that were much pleased and delighted by such accidents upon this stage would not be grieved by the same things in a greater stage and affliction.

Here you see what is the end of all such things, and that even they that cry out so mournfully to Cithaeron[16], must bear them for all their cries and exclamations, as well as others. And in truth many good things are spoken by these poets. For example, this is an excellent passage: "But if it is so that I and my two children are neglected by the gods, they have some reason even for that."

And again, "It will but little avail you to storm and rage against the things themselves." Again, "To reap one's life as ripe grain." Whatever else is to be found in them, that is of the same kind.

After the tragedy, the ancient comedy was brought in, which had the liberty to inveigh against personal vices, being therefore through this her freedom and liberty of speech of very good use and effect. It restrained men from pride and arrogance.

To which end it was that Diogenes took also the same liberty. After these, what were either the Middle, or New Comedy admitted for, but merely, (or for the most part at least) for the delight and pleasure of curious and excellent imitation?

"It will steal away; look to it." Why, no man denies that these also have some good things that may be one: but the whole drift and foundation of that kind of dramatic poetry, what is it else, but as we have said?

▼

How clearly does it appear to you that no other course of your life could fit a true philosopher's practice better than this very course that you are now already in?

▼

A branch cut off from the continuity of that which was next to it must be cut off from the whole tree. A man that is divided from another man is divided from the whole society. A branch is cut off by another, but he that hates and is averse cuts himself off from his neighbor. He doesn't know that at the same time he divides himself from the whole body, or corporation.

But herein is the gift and mercy of God, the Author of this society, in that, once cut off we may grow together and become a part of the whole again.

But if this happens, often the misery is that the further a man is run in this division, the harder he is to be reunited and restored again.

However the branch which, once cut of afterwards was grafted in, gardeners can tell you is not like that which sprouted together at first, and still continued in the unity of the body.

▼

Grow together like fellow branches in the matter of good correspondence and affection, but not in matter of opinions. As it is not in the power of those that will oppose you in your right courses to divert you from your good action, so neither let it be to divert you from your good affection towards them.

But take care to keep yourself constant in both; both in a right judgment and action, and in true meekness towards them that either endeavor to hinder you, or at least will be displeased with you for what you have done.

For to fail in either (either in the one to give over for fear, or in the other to forsake your natural affection towards him, who by nature is both your friend and your kinsman) is equally base, and much savoring of the disposition of a cowardly fugitive soldier.

157

▼

It is not possible that any nature should be inferior to an area, since all areas imitate nature. If this is so, that the most perfect and general nature of all natures should in her operation, come short of the skill of areas is most improbable. Now it is common to all areas to make that which is worse, better. Much more then does the common nature do the same.

This is the first ground of justice. From justice all other virtues have their existence. For justice cannot be preserved, if either we settle our minds and affections upon worldly things, or be apt to be deceived, or rash, and inconstant.

▼

The things themselves which you are put to so much trouble either to get or to avoid don't come to you themselves, but you in a manner go to. Let your own judgment and opinion concerning those things be at rest. As for the things themselves, they stand still and quiet, without any noise or stir at all, and so shall all pursuing and flying cease.

▼

It is the soul, as Empedocles likens it, like a sphere or globe, when she is all of one form and figure. When she neither greedily stretches herself out to anything, nor basely contracts herself, or lies flat and dejected; but shines with all light, whereby she sees and beholds the true nature, both that of the universe and her own in particular.

Empedocles

▼

Will any hold me in contempt? let him look to that, upon what grounds does he does it. My care shall be that I may never be found either doing or speaking anything that truly deserves contempt. Will any hate me? let him look to that.

I for my part will be kind and loving to all, and even to him that hates me, whoever he is, I will be ready to show his error. Not by way of criticism or ostentation of my patience, but ingenuously and meekly, such as was that famous Phocion, if it is that he didn't dissemble.

For it is inwardly that these things must be. The gods who look inwardly, and not upon the outward appearance, may behold a man truly free from all indignation and grief. For what hurt can it be to you whatever any other man does, as long as you may do that which is proper and suitable to your own nature?

Will you, a man wholly appointed to be both what, and as the common good shall require, accept that which is now seasonable to the nature of the universe?

▼

They look at one another with contempt, and yet they seek to please one another. And while they seek to surpass one another in worldly pomp and greatness, they most debase and prostitute themselves in their better part to one another.

▼

How rotten and insincere is anyone who says "I am resolved to carry myself hereafter towards you with all ingenuity and simplicity." Oh, man, what do you mean?! What does this profession of yours need? The thing itself will show it. It ought to be written on your forehead.

No sooner is your voice heard than your countenance must be able to show what is in your mind; even as he that is loved knows presently by the looks of his sweetheart what is in her mind.

Such must he be for all the world that is truly simple and good, as he whose armpits are offensive, that whoever stands by him, as soon as ever he comes near him may smell him whether he wants to or not. But the affectation of simplicity is in no way laudable.

There is nothing more shameful than perfidious friendship. That must be avoided above all things. However, true goodness, simplicity, and kindness cannot be so hidden, but that as we have already said in the very eyes and countenance they will show themselves.

To live happily is an inward power of the soul, when she is affected with indifference towards those things that are by their nature indifferent. To be thus affected she must consider all worldly objects both divided and whole, remembering that no object can of itself beget any opinion in us. Neither can it come to us but stands still and quiet, but that we ourselves beget, and as it were print in ourselves opinions concerning them.

Now, it is in our power not to print them; and if they creep in and lurk in some corner, it is in our power to wipe them off. Remembering moreover, that this care and circumspection of yours is to continue but for a while, and then your life will be at an end.

And what should hinder, but that you may do well with all these things? For if they are according to nature, rejoice in them, and let them be pleasing and acceptable to you.

But if they are against nature, seek that which is according to your own nature, and whether it is for your credit or not, use all possible speed for the attainment of it. For no one ought to be blamed for seeking their own good and happiness.

▼

Of everything you must consider from where it came, what it consists of, and what it will be changed into. What will be the nature of it, or what it will be like when it is changed? Consider that it can suffer no harm by this change.

And as for other men's foolishness or wickedness, that it may not trouble and grieve you; first generally this, what reference do I have to these? And that we are all born for one another's good, then more particularly after another consideration, as a ram is first in a flock of sheep, and a bull in a herd of cattle, so I am born to rule over them.

Begin yet higher, even from this: if atoms are not the beginning of all things, than which to believe nothing can be more absurd, then we must grant that there is a nature that governs the universe. If there is such a nature, then all worse things are made for the better's sake; and all better for one another's sake.

Secondly, what manner of men they are, at board, and upon their beds, and so forth. But above all things, how they are forced by their opinions that they hold to do what they do. Even those things that they do, with what pride and self-conceit they do them.

Thirdly, that if they do these things correctly, you have no reason to be grieved. But if not correctly, it must be that they do them against their wills, and through mere ignorance. For as, according to Plato's opinion, no soul willingly errs, so by consequent neither does it do anything otherwise than it should, but against her will.

Therefore they are grieved whenever they hear themselves charged, either of injustice or immorality, or covetousness, or in general, of any injurious kind of dealing towards their neighbors.

Fourthly, that you yourself transgress in many things, and are even such as they are. And though perchance you forbear the very act of some sins, yet have you in yourself a habitual disposition to them, but that either through fear, or vainglory, or some such other ambitious foolish respect, you are restrained.

Fifthly, that whether they have sinned or not, you do not understand perfectly. For many things are done by way of discreet policy; and generally a man must know many things first, before he is truly and judiciously able to judge of another man's action.

Sixthly, that whenever you do take on grievously, or make great woe, little do you remember then that a man's life is but for a moment of time, and that within a while we shall all be in our graves.

Seventhly, that it is not the sins and transgressions themselves that trouble us properly, for they have their existence in their minds and understandings only that commit them, but our own opinions concerning those sins. Remove then, and be content to part with that conceit of yours that it is a grievous thing, and you have removed your anger.

But how should I remove it? How? Reasoning with yourself that it is not shameful. For if that which is shameful, is not the only true evil that is, you also will be driven while you follow the common instinct of nature to avoid that which is evil, to commit many unjust things, and to become a thief, and anything, that will make to the attainment of your intended worldly ends.

Eighthly, how many things may and do often follow upon such fits of anger and grief? They are far more grievous in themselves, than those very things which we are so grieved or angry for.

Ninthly, that meekness is a thing unconquerable, if it is true and natural, and not affected or hypocritical. For how shall even the most fierce and malicious that you will conceive of be able to hold on against you if you will still continue meek and loving to him, and that even at that time, when he is about to do you wrong, you will be well disposed, and in good temper, with all meekness to teach him, and to instruct him better?

As for example, "My son, we were not born for this, to hurt and annoy one another. It will be your hurt, not mine, my son." And so to show him forcibly and fully that it is so indeed, and that neither bees do it to one another, nor any other creatures that are naturally sociable.

But you must do this, not scoffing, not by way of accusation, but tenderly and without any harshness of words. Neither must you do it by way of exercise, or ostentation, that they that are by and hear you may admire you, but so always that nobody is privy to it but he alone. Yes, even though there are more present at the same time.

See that you remember these nine particular heads, as so many gifts from the Muses, well. Begin one day while you are yet alive to be a man indeed. But on the other side you must take heed, as much to flatter them, as to be angry with them, for both are equally uncharitable and equally hurtful.

And in your passions, take it presently to your consideration that to be angry is not the part of a man, but that to be meek and gentle, as it savors of more humanity, so of more manhood. That in this there is strength and nerves, or vigor and fortitude, whereof anger and indignation is altogether void. For the nearer everything is to dispassionateness, the nearer it is to power.

And as grief proceeds from weakness, so does anger. For both, both he that is angry and that grieves have received a wound, and cowardly have as it were yielded themselves to their affections.

If you will have a tenth also, receive this tenth gift from Hercules the guide and leader of the Muses, that is a madman's part to look that there should be no wicked men in the world, because it is impossible. Now for a man to brook well enough, that there should be wicked men in the world, but not to endure that any should transgress against himself is against all equity, and indeed tyrannical.

▼

Four several dispositions or inclinations there are of the mind and understanding, which to be aware of you must carefully observe, and whenever you do discover them you must rectify them, saying to yourself concerning every one of them, this imagination is not necessary; this is uncharitable.

This you will speak as another man's slave, or instrument, than which nothing can be more senseless and absurd. For the fourth, you will sharply check and upbraid yourself, for that you suffer that more divine part in you to become subject and obnoxious to that more ignoble part of your body, and the gross lusts thereof.

▼

What portion either of air or fire is there in you, although by nature it tends upwards? It nevertheless submits to the ordinance of the universe, abiding here below in this mixed body. So whatever is in you, either earthy or humid, although by nature it tends downwards, yet is it against its nature both raised upwards, and standing, or consistent.

So obedient are even the elements themselves to the universe, abiding patiently wherever (though against their nature) they are placed, until the sound as it were of their retreat and separation. Is it not a grievous thing then, that your reasonable part only should be disobedient, and should not endure to keep its place. Yes, though it is nothing joined that is contrary to it, but only that which is according to its nature?

For we cannot say of it when it is disobedient, as we say of the fire, or air, that it tends upwards towards its proper element, for then it goes quite the contrary way. For the motion of the mind to any injustice, or incontinence, or to sorrow, or to fear, is nothing else but a separation from nature.

Also when the mind is grieved for anything that has happened by the divine providence, then does it likewise forsake its own place. For it was ordained to holiness and godliness, which specially consist in a humble submission to God and His providence in all things, as well as to justice. These also are part of those duties, which as naturally sociable we are bound to, and without which we cannot happily converse one with another. Yes, and the very ground and fountain indeed of all just actions.

▼

He that doesn't always have one and the same general end as long as he lives can't possibly always be one and the same man. But this will not suffice except that you also add what ought to be this general end.

For as the general conceit and apprehension of all those things which upon no certain ground are by the greater part of men deemed good, cannot be uniform and agreeable, but that only which is limited and restrained by some certain proprieties and conditions, as of community.

Nothing is conceived of as good which is not commonly

and publicly good. So must the end also be that we propose to ourselves, be common and sociable. For he who directs all his own private motions and purposes to that end, all his actions will be agreeable and uniform. By that means he will still be the same man.

▼

Remember the fable of the country mouse and the city mouse, and the great fright and terror that this was put into them.[17]

▼

Socrates was accustomed to call the common conceits and opinions of men "the common bugbears of the world, the proper terror of silly children."

▼

The Lacedaemonians at their public spectacles were accustomed to appoint seats and forms for their strangers in the shade, they themselves were content to sit anywhere.

▼

What Socrates answered to Perdiccas, why he didn't come to him, lest of all deaths I should die the worst kind of death, said he. That is, not able to requite the good that has been done to me.

▼

In the ancient mystical letters of the Ephesians[19], there was an item that a man should always have in his mind some one or another of the ancient worthies.

▼

The first thing The Pythagoreans[18] were at times used to do in the morning was to look up to the sky, to put themselves in mind of them who constantly and invariably performed their task. Also to put themselves in mind of orderliness, or good order, and of purity, and of naked simplicity. For no star or planet has any cover before it.

▼

How Socrates looked, when he had to gird himself with a skin, Xanthippe his wife having taken away his clothes, and carried them abroad with her, and what he said to his fellows and friends, who were ashamed; and out of respect to him, retired themselves when they saw him thus decked.

▼

In the matter of writing or reading you must be taught before you can do either. It is much more in the matter of life. "For you are born a mere slave to your senses and brutish affections," destitute without teaching of all true knowledge and sound reason.

▼

"My heart smiled within me; They will accuse even virtue herself; with heinous and opprobrious words."

▼

As they that long after figs in winter when they cannot be had, so are they that long after children before they are granted them.

▼

"As often as a father kisses his child he should say secretly with himself," said Epictetus, "tomorrow perchance shall he die." But these words are ominous. No ominous words (said he) that signify anything that is natural; in very truth and deed not more ominous than this, "to cut down grapes when they are ripe."

Green grapes, ripe grapes, dried grapes, or raisins; so many changes and mutations of one thing, not into that which was not absolute, but rather so many several changes and mutations, not into that which has no being at all, but into that which is not yet in being.

▼

"Of the free will there is no thief or robber" out

of Epictetus, whose is this also: "That we should find a certain area and method of assenting; and that we should always observe with great care and heed the inclinations of our minds that they may always be with their due restraint and reservation, always charitable, and according to the true worth of every present object.

"And as for earnest longing, that we should altogether avoid it and to be averse only to those things that wholly depend of our own wills. It is not about ordinary petty matters, believe it, that all our strife and contention is, but whether, with the vulgar, we should be mad, or by the help of philosophy wise and sober," said he.

Socrates said, "What will you have? The souls of reasonable or unreasonable creatures? Of reasonable. But what? Of those whose reason is sound and perfect? Or of those whose reason is vitiated and corrupted? Of those whose reason is sound and perfect. Then why not work for such? Because we have them already. What then do you so strive and contend between yourself?"

▲

Chapter Twelve
Opinions of Others

Whatever you aspire to from now on, you may even now enjoy and possess if you don't envy yourself of your own happiness. And that will be, if you will forget all that is past, and for the future refer yourself wholly to the Divine Providence, and will bend and apply all your present thoughts and intentions to holiness and righteousness.

To holiness, in accepting willingly whatever is sent by the Divine Providence, as being that which the nature of the universe has appointed to you, which also has appointed you for that, whatever it is.

To righteousness, in speaking the truth freely, and without ambiguity; and in doing all things justly and discreetly. Now, in this good course don't let other men's either wickedness, or opinion, or voice, hinder you; no, nor the sense of your pampered mass of flesh.

Let that which suffers look to itself. If therefore whenever the time of your departing shall come, you will readily leave all things, and will respect your mind only, and that divine part of you, and this shall be your only fear, not that some time or other you will cease to live, but you will never begin to live according to nature. Then will you be a man indeed, worthy of that world from which you had your beginning; then will you cease to be a stranger in your country, and to wonder at those things that happen daily as things strange and unexpected, and anxiously to depend of diverse things that are not in your power.

▼

God beholds our minds and understandings, bare and naked from these material vessels, and outsides, and all earthly dross. For with His simple and pure understanding, He pierces into our inmost and purest parts, which from His, as it were by a water pipe and channel first flowed and issued.

This if you also will use to do, you will rid yourself of

that manifold luggage, wherewith you are round about encumbered. For he that regards neither his body nor his clothing nor his dwelling, nor any such external furniture must gain to himself great rest and ease. Three things there are in all which you consist of; your body, your life, and your mind.

Of these the two former, are so far for you, as that you are bound to take care for them. But the third alone is that which is properly yours. If then you will separate from yourself, that is from your mind, whatever other men either do or say, or whatever you yourself have heretofore either done or said; and all troublesome thoughts concerning the future, and whatever, (as either belonging to your body or life) is without the jurisdiction of your own will, and whatever in the ordinary course of human chances and accidents happens to you; so that your mind (keeping herself loose and free from all outward coincidental entanglements; always in a readiness to depart) shall live by herself, and to herself, doing that which is just, accepting whatever happens, and always speaking the truth.

If, I say, you will separate from your mind whatever by sympathy might adhere to it, and all time both past and future, and will make yourself in all points and respects like Empedocles' allegorical sphere[20], "all round and circular," and will no longer think of life than that which is now present: then you will be truly able to pass the remainder of your days without troubles and distractions; nobly and generously disposed, and in good favor and correspondence with that spirit which is within you.

▼

I have often wondered how it should have come to pass that every man loving himself best should more regard other men's opinions concerning himself than his own. For if any God or grave master standing by should command any of us to think nothing by himself but what he should presently speak out, no man would be able to endure it, though but for one day. Thus do we fear more what our neighbors will think of us than what we ourselves do.

▼

How did it come to pass that the gods, having ordered all other things so well and so lovingly, should only overlook this one thing, that whereas there have been some very good men that have made many covenants, as it were with God and by many holy actions and outward services, contracted a kind of familiarity with Him; that once these men are dead, should never be restored to life, but be extinct forever.

But this you may be sure of, that this (if it is so indeed) would never have been so ordered by the gods had it been fit otherwise. For certainly it was possible, had it been more just so and had it been according to nature, the nature of the universe would easily have borne it.

But now because it is not so, (if that is not so indeed) be therefore confident that it was not fit, it should be so for you see yourself, that now seeking after this matter, how freely you argue and contest with God.

But were not the gods both just and good in the highest degree, you dare not reason with them. Now if they are just and good, it could not be that in the creation of the world they should either unjustly or unreasonably oversee anything.

▼

Use yourself even for those things that you despair of at first. For the left hand, which for the most part lies idle because it's not used, yet it holds the bridle with more strength than the right, because it's used to it.

▼

Let these be the objects of your ordinary meditation—to consider what manner of men both for soul and body we ought to be whenever death surprises us, the shortness of this our mortal life, the immense vastness of the time that has been before and will be after us, the frailty of every worldly material object. All these things to consider, and behold clearly in themselves, all disguise of the external outside being removed and taken away.

Again, consider the efficient causes of all things, the proper ends and references of all actions, what pain is in itself, what pleasure, what death, what fame or honor, how every man is the true and proper ground of his own rest and tranquility, and that no man can truly be hindered by any other.

That all is but conceit and opinion.

As for the use of your dogma, you must carry yourself in the practice of them, rather like to a *pancratiastes*, or one that at the same time both fights and wrestles with hands and feet rather than like a gladiator. For if the gladiator loses the sword that he fights with, he is gone, whereas the other has still his hand free, which he may easily turn and manage at his will.

▼

You must behold and consider all worldly things, dividing them into matter, form, and reference, or their proper end.

▼

How happy is a man that has been granted this power, that he needs not do anything but what God shall approve, and that he may embrace contentedly, whatever God sends to him?

▼

Whatever happens in the ordinary course and consequence of natural events, neither the gods, (for it is not possible that they either wittingly or unwittingly should do anything amiss) nor men, (for it is through ignorance, and therefore against their wills that they do anything amiss) must be accused. None then must be accused.

▼

How ridiculous and strange is he that wonders about anything that happens in this life in the ordinary course of nature!

▼

Either fate (and that either an absolute necessity, and

171

unavoidable decree; or a forgiving and flexible Providence), or all is a mere casual confusion, void of all order and government. If it is an absolute and unavoidable necessity, why do you resist?

If a gentle and persuadable Providence, make yourself worthy of the divine help and assistance.

If all is mere confusion without any moderator, or governor, then you have reason to congratulate yourself; that in such a general flood of confusion, you yourself have obtained a reasonable faculty, whereby you may govern your own life and actions.

But if you are carried away with the flood, it must be your body perchance, or your life, or some other thing that belongs to them that is carried away. Your mind and understanding cannot.

Or should it be so, that the light of a candle indeed is still bright until it's put out, and should truth, and righteousness, and temperance cease to shine in you while you yourself have any being?

▼

At the conceit and apprehension that such and such a one has sinned, thus reason with yourself: What do I know whether this be a sin indeed, as it seems to be?

But if it is, what do I know but that he himself has already condemned himself for it? And that is all one as if a man should scratch and tear his own face, an object of compassion rather than of anger.

Again, that he that would not have a vicious man to sin, is like to him that would not have moisture in the fig, nor children to grow nor a horse to neigh, nor anything else that in the course of nature is necessary. For what shall he do that has such a habit? If you therefore are powerful and eloquent, remedy it if you can.

▼

If it isn't fitting, don't do it. If it isn't true, don't say it.

Ever maintain your own purpose and resolution, free from all compulsion and necessity.

▼

Of everything that presents itself to you, consider what the true nature of it is, and unfold it, as it were, by dividing it into that which is formal: that which is material, the true use or end of it, and the just time that it is appointed to last.

▼

It is high time for you to understand that there is something in you better and more divine than either your passions or your sensual appetites and affections. What is now the object of my mind, is it fear, or suspicion, or lust, or any such thing?

To do nothing rashly without some certain end; let that be your first care. The next, to have no other end than the common good. For, alas! Yet a little while, and you are no more: no more will any, either of those things that now you see, or of those men that now are living, be any more. For all things are by nature appointed soon to be changed, turned, and corrupted, that other things might succeed in their room.

▼

Remember that all is but opinion, and all opinion depends on the mind. Take your opinion away, and then as a ship that has stricken in within the arms and mouth of the harbor, a present calm; all things safe and steady: a bay, not capable of any storms and tempests, as the poet has it.

▼

No operation ceasing for a while, whatever it is, can be truly said to suffer any evil because it is at an end. Neither can he that is the author of that operation; for this very respect, because his operation is at an end, be said to suffer any evil.

Likewise then, neither can the whole body of all our actions (which is our life) if in time it cease, be said to suffer any evil for this very reason, because it is at an end; nor he truly be said to have been ill affected, that did put a period to this series of actions.

Now this time or certain period depends on the determination of nature: sometimes of particular nature, as when a man dies old; but of nature in general, however; the parts thus changing one after another, the whole world still continues fresh and new.

Now that is ever best and most seasonable which is for the good of the whole. Thus it appears that death of itself can neither be hurtful to any in particular, because it is not a shameful thing (for neither is it a thing that depends of our own will, nor of itself contrary to the common good) and generally, as it is both expedient and seasonable to the whole, that in that respect it must be good.

It is that also, which is brought to us by the order and appointment of the Divine Providence, so that he whose will and mind in these things runs along with the Divine ordinance, and by this concurrence of his will and mind with the Divine Providence, is led and driven along, as it were by God Himself; may truly be termed and esteemed the divinely led and inspired.

▼

There are three things you must have always in a readiness. First, concerning your own actions, whether you do nothing either idly or otherwise than justice and equity require. Concerning those things that happen to you externally, that either they happen to you by chance, or by providence; of which to accuse either two is equally against reason.

Secondly, while our bodies are rude and imperfect until they are animated, and from their animation until their expiration of what things they are compounded, and into what things they shall be dissolved.

Thirdly, how vain all things will appear to you when, from on high as it were, looking down you will contemplate all things on the earth, and the wonderful mutability that they are subject to, considering withal the infinite both greatness and variety of things aerial and things celestial that are round about it.

And that as often as you will behold them, you will still see the same, as the same things, so the same shortness of continuance of all those things. And, behold, these be the things that we are so proud and puffed up for.

▼

Cast away your opinion and you are safe. And what is it that hinders you from casting of it away? When you are grieved at anything, have you forgotten that all things happen according to the nature of the universe? That it only concerns he who is in fault, and moreover, that what is now done, is that which from ever has been done in the world, and will ever be done, and is now done everywhere.

How nearly all men are allied one to another by a kindred not of blood, nor of seed, but of the same mind. You have also forgotten that every man's mind partakes of the Deity, and issues from there; and that no man can properly call anything his own, no not his son, nor his body, nor his life; for that they all proceed from that One who is the giver of all things.

That all things are but opinion, that no man lives properly, but that very instant of time which is now present. And therefore that no man, whenever he dies, can properly be said to lose any more than an instant of time.

▼

Let your thoughts ever run upon them who, once for some one thing or other, were moved with extraordinary indignation; who were once in the highest pitch of either honor, or calamity; or mutual hatred and enmity; or of any other fortune or condition whatever.

Then consider what's now become of all those things. All is turned to smoke; all to ashes, and a mere fable; and perchance not so much as a fable.

As also whatever is of this nature, as Fabius Catulinus in the field; Lucius Lupus, and Stertinius, at Baiae Tiberius at Caprem. and Velius Rufus, and all such examples of vehement prosecution in worldly matters. Let these also run in your mind at the same time; and how vile every object of such earnest and vehement prosecution is, and how much more agreeable to true philosophy it is for a man to carry himself in every matter that offers itself; justly, and moderately, as one that follows the gods with all simplicity.

For a man to be proud and high conceited, that he is not proud and high conceited, is of all kind of pride and presumption the most intolerable.

▼

To them that ask you, "Where have you seen the gods, or how do you know with certainty that there are gods, that you are so devout in their worship?"

I answer first of all, that even to the very eye they are in some manner visible and apparent. Secondly, neither have I ever seen my own soul, and yet I respect and honor it.

So then for the gods, by the daily experience that I have of their power and providence towards myself and others, I know certainly that they are, and therefore worship them.

▼

Herein consists happiness of life: for a man to know thoroughly the true nature of everything. What is its matter? What is the form of it? With all his heart and soul, ever is he to do that which is just, and to speak the truth.

What then remains but to enjoy your life in a course and coherence of good actions, one upon another immediately succeeding, and never interrupted, though for never so little a while?

▼

There is but one light of the sun, though it is intercepted by walls and mountains, and a thousand other objects. There is but only common substance of the whole world, though it is concluded and restrained into several different bodies, in infinite number.

There is but one common soul, though divided into innumerable particular essences and natures. So is there but

176

one common intellectual soul, though it seems to be divided.

And as for all other parts of those generals which we have mentioned, as either sensitive souls or subjects, these of themselves (as naturally irrational) have no common mutual reference to one another, though many of them contain a mind, or reasonable faculty in them, whereby they are ruled and governed.

But of every reasonable mind, this the particular nature, that it has reference to whatever is of her own kind, and desires to be united. Neither can this common affection, or mutual unity and correspondence, be intercepted or divided, or confined to particulars as those other common things are.

▼

What do you desire? To live long. What? To enjoy the operations of a sensitive soul; or of the appetitive faculty? or would you grow, and then decrease again? Would you long be able to talk, to think and reason with yourself?

Which of all these seems to your a worthy object of your desire? Now if of all these you find that they are but little worth in themselves, proceed on to the last, which is, in all things to follow God and reason. But for a man to grieve that by death he shall be deprived of any of these things is both against God and reason.

▼

What a small portion of vast and infinite eternity it is that is allowed to every one of us, and how soon it vanishes into the general age of the world. Of the common substance, and of the common soul also what a small portion is allotted to us. In what a little clod of the whole earth (as it were) it is that you crawl.

After you will rightly have considered these things with yourself, fancy not anything else in the world any more to be of any weight and moment but this, to do that only which your own nature requires; and to conform yourself to that which the common nature affords.

▼

What is the present state of my understanding? For herein lies all indeed. As for all other things, they are without the compass of my own will. If without the compass of my will, then are they as dead things to me, and as it were, mere smoke.

▼

To stir up a man to the contempt of death, this among other things, is of good power and efficacy, that even they who esteemed pleasure to be happiness, and pain misery, did nevertheless many of them contemn death as much as any. And can death be terrible to him to whom that only seems good, which in the ordinary course of nature is seasonable? To him, whether his actions be many or few, so they be all good, is all one; and who whether he beholds the things of the world being always the same either for many years, or for few years only, is altogether indifferent?

Oh, man! You have lived as a citizen, and conversed in this great city, the world. Whether just for so many years or not, what is it to you? You have lived, you may be sure, as long as the laws and orders of the city required; which may be the common comfort of all.

Why then should it be grievous to you, if not a tyrant, nor an unjust judge, but the same nature that brought you in, does now send your out of the world? As if the praetor should fairly dismiss him from the stage whom he had taken in to act a while.

Oh, but the play is not yet at an end, there are but three acts yet acted of it? You have well said. For in matter of life, three acts is the whole play. Now to set a certain time to every man's acting, belongs to him only, who as first he was of your composition, so is now the cause of your dissolution.

As for yourself; you have to do with neither. Go your ways then well pleased and contented, for so is He that dismisses you.

▲

Notes

1 (Page 4): Diognetus was one of Marcus' teachers, a painting master who proved particularly influential, seemingly to have converted Marcus to the philosophic way of life. In April 132, at the behest of Diognetus, Marcus took up the dress and habits of the philosopher. He studied while wearing a rough Greek cloak, and would sleep on the ground until his mother convinced him to sleep on a bed.

2 (Page 5): Quintus Junius Rusticus was a Stoic philosopher and one of Marcus teachers, whom he treated with the utmost respect and honor.

Rusticus held the political positions of Suffect consul in 133 and Consul ordinarius in 162. He served as urban prefect of Rome between 162 and 168. In this role he is notable for presiding over the trial of the Christian theologian Justin Martyr, which ended with Justin's conviction and execution, illustrated on page 4.

3 (Page 5): The Sophists were paid teachers of philosophy and rhetoric, who used specious reasoning and were skeptical of morals.

Sophistry is using fallacious arguments designed to fool.

Sophistication is having a great deal of knowledge of fashion and culture; in essence, fakery. Sophism is the modern prevailing philosophy. People today are more concerned with looks than use, the adage "form follows function" having fallen out of favor long ago.

4 (Page 5): Apollonius was one of Marcus' teachers who first introduced him to philosophy.

5 (Page 6): Sextus of Chaeronea was a philosopher, a nephew or grandson of Plutarch, and one of the teachers of the

emperor Marcus Aurelius.

6 (Page 7): Fronto was Marcus' teacher in Latin oratory before he discovered philosophy. Fronto hated that fact. "It is better never to have touched the teaching of philosophy... than to have tasted it superficially, with the edge of the lips, as the saying is."

7 (Page 8): Claudius Maximus was a Roman politician, a Stoic philosopher, and a teacher of Marcus Aurelius. No works by him are known to exist.

8 (Page 40): Cecrops was a mythical king of Attica which derived from him its name Cecropia, having previously borne the name of Acte or Actice (from Actaeus). He was the founder and the first king of Athens itself though preceded in the region by the earth-born king Actaeus of Attica. Cecrops was a culture hero, teaching the Athenians marriage, reading and writing, and ceremonial burial.

8 (Page 42): Vespasian was Roman emperor from 69 to 79. The fourth and last in the Year of the Four Emperors, he founded the Flavian dynasty that ruled the Empire for 27 years.

9 (Page 43): Trajan was Roman emperor from 98 to 117. Officially declared by the Senate *optimus princeps* ("best ruler"), Trajan is remembered as a successful soldier-emperor who presided over the greatest military expansion in Roman history, leading the empire to attain its maximum territorial extent by the time of his death. He is also known for his philanthropic rule, overseeing extensive public building programs and implementing social welfare policies, which earned him his enduring reputation as the second of the Five Good Emperors, who presided over an era of peace and prosperity in the Mediterranean world.

10 (Page 46): Heraclitus of Ephesus was an Ancient Greek, pre-Socratic, Ionian philosopher and a native of the city of Ephesus, which was then part of the Persian Empire.

His appreciation for wordplay and oracular expressions, as well as paradoxical elements in his philosophy, earned him the epithet "The Obscure" from antiquity. He wrote a single work, *On Nature*, only fragments of which have survived, increasing the obscurity associated with his life and philosophy. Heraclitus's cryptic utterances have been the subject of numerous interpretations. He has been seen as a "material monist" or a process philosopher; a scientific cosmologist, a metaphysician and a religious thinker; an empiricist, a rationalist, a mystic; a conventional thinker and a revolutionary; a developer of logic—one who denied the law of non-contradiction; the first genuine philosopher and an anti-intellectual obscurantist.

11 (Page 69): The writings of Crates are lost. Crates of Thebes was a Cynic philosopher who gave away his money to live a life of poverty on the streets of Athens. Respected by the people of Athens, he is remembered for being the teacher of Zeno of Citium, the founder of Stoicism. Various fragments of Crates' teachings survive, including his description of the ideal Cynic state.

Xenocrates of Chalcedon was a Greek philosopher, mathematician, and leader of the Platonic Academy from 339 to 314 BC. His teachings followed those of Plato, which he attempted to define more closely, often with mathematical elements. He distinguished three forms of being: the sensible, the intelligible, and a third compounded of the two, to which correspond respectively, sense, intellect and opinion. He considered unity and duality to be gods which rule the universe, and the soul a self-moving number. God pervades all things, and there are demonical powers, intermediate between the divine and the mortal, which consist in conditions of the soul. He held that mathematical objects and the Platonic Ideas are identical, unlike Plato who distinguished them. In ethics, he taught that virtue produces happiness, but external goods can minister to it and enable it to effect its purpose.

12 (Page 69): It was only a century ago that we discovered that the universe was thirteen or fourteen billion years old, and that the Earth itself is four billion. Before Edwin Hubble discovered that the universe was expanding, it had been assumed that it was timeless.

13 (Page 74): Antoninus Pius was Marcus' legal stepfather, although his mother and grandfather raised Marcus. Antonius was the emperor before Marcus.

14 (Page 102): He didn't want to become emperor. His biographer wrote that he was "compelled" to take imperial power. With his preference for the philosophic life, he found the imperial office unappealing. His training as a Stoic, however, had made the choice clear to him that it was his duty.

15 (Page 131): Gold and silver, rather than being the "Earth's feces", were actually expelled from exploding stars and deposited on Earth, but there was no way anyone in antiquity could know that.

16 (Page 156): Cithaeron is a mountain and mountain range about ten miles long in central Greece. The range is the physical boundary between Boeotia in the north and Attica in the south.

17 (Page 165): In the original tale, a proud town mouse visits his cousin in the country. The country mouse offers the city mouse a meal of simple country cuisine, at which the visitor scoffs and invites the country mouse back to the city for a taste of the "fine life" and the two cousins dine on white bread and other fine foods. But their rich feast is interrupted

by a cat which forces the rodent cousins to abandon their meal and retreat back into their mouse hole for safety. Town mouse tells country mouse that the cat killed his mother and father and that he is frequently the target of attacks. After hearing this, the country mouse decides to return home, preferring security to opulence or, as the 13th-century preacher Odo of Cheriton phrased it, "I'd rather gnaw a bean than be gnawed by continual fear".

18 (Page 165): Pythagoreanism originated in the 6th century BC, based on the teachings and beliefs held by Pythagoras and his followers, the Pythagoreans.

Pythagoras was already in ancient times well known for the mathematical achievement of the Pythagorean theorem. Pythagoras had been credited with discovering that in a right-angled triangle the square of the hypotenuse is equal to the sum of the squares of the other two sides. In ancient times Pythagoras was also noted for his discovery that music had mathematical foundations. Antique sources that credit Pythagoras as the philosopher who first discovered music intervals also credit him as the inventor of the monochord, a straight rod on which a string and a movable bridge could be used to demonstrate the relationship of musical intervals.

19 (Page 165): Ephesus was an ancient Greek city on the coast of Ionia, about 1.8 miles southwest of present-day Selçuk in İzmir Province, Turkey. It was built in the 10th century BC on the site of the former Arzawan capital by Attic and Ionian Greek colonists. During the Classical Greek era it was one of the twelve cities of the Ionian League.

20 (Page 169): Empedocles maintained that as the best and original state, there was a time when the pure elements and the two powers co-existed in a condition of rest and inertness in the form of a sphere. The elements existed together in their purity, without mixture and separation, and

the uniting power of Love predominated in the sphere: the separating power of Strife guarded the extreme edges of the sphere. Since that time, strife gained more sway and the bond which kept the pure elementary substances together in the sphere was dissolved. The elements became the world of phenomena we see today, full of contrasts and oppositions, operated on by both Love and Strife. The sphere of Empedocles being the embodiment of pure existence is the embodiment or representative of God. Empedocles assumed a cyclical universe whereby the elements return and prepare the formation of the sphere for the next period of the universe.